BUILD WEALTH TAX FREE

THE PROFIT FORMULA

How to Create Massive Returns
TAX-FREE Using Michael Poggi's
Turn-Key Investing
Formulas

MICHAEL POGGI

POGGI WEALTH
INSTITUTE

BUILD WEALTH TAX FREE
The Profit Formula
by Michael Poggi, Investor/Speaker
©2011 Michael Poggi - Poggi Wealth Institute
All Rights Reserved

ISBN#: 978-0-615-55581-2

Published By:
Poggi Publishing Company
11365 Earnest Blvd. Davie, FL 33325
(954) 306-3586

www.MichaelPoggi.com

TABLE OF CONTENTS

FOREWORD

You can't fly a kite unless you go against the wind and
have a weight to keep it from turning a somersault.
The same with man. No man will succeed unless he is
ready to face and overcome difficulties and
is prepared to assume responsibilities.

William J.H. Boetcker

When I hear somebody sigh that Life is hard,
I am always tempted to ask, Compared to what?

Sydney J. Harris

It is surmounting difficulties that makes heroes.

Louis Pasteur

AUTHOR'S NOTE

Did you know there's a secret IRS regulation you can use to get rich, and never pay taxes? It's true—and even better you can also use this "secret regulation" to pass your tax-free riches onto your children and grandchildren.

No, this isn't some goofy tax protest fantasy or Caribbean off-shore scheme designed to cheat the IRS, nor is it some vague loophole the IRS hasn't yet closed. All of those things will eventually get you in trouble, even land you in jail. What I'm about to reveal to you is perfectly legal, and in fact encouraged by the United States government itself.

– Michael Poggi

ACKNOWLEDGMENTS

First and foremost, I want to thank my parents and my brother who have supported me, encouraged me, motivated me, and loved me unconditionally all my life. They also have inspired me to be the best I can be. They taught me to be an over achiever and a big giver. They have taught me to love people and animals with all my heart! They held me up when I was down and always gave me the tools I needed to be successful. I am so grateful for all of their support and love over the last 45 years. I love my family with all my heart and I thank you with every ounce of my being.

I would like to express my appreciation to all my staff, both past and present, for their continued dedication to the pursuit of excellence in investing.

And, perhaps most importantly, I want to thank my clients for their on-going support, confidence and collaboration through the investment process. Together, we have been able to translate a common vision into reality.

OPENING WORDS

You can do it if you believe you can.
You control your destiny.

There are many things you cannot control, but you can control the only things that really matter: Your mind and your attitude. External forces have very little to do with success. Those who program themselves for success find a way to succeed even in the most difficult of circumstances. Solutions to most problems come from one source and one source alone: Yourself.

Living life to the fullest is a lot like shooting the rapids in a rubber raft. Once you've made the commitment, it's difficult to change your mind, turn around, and paddle upstream to placid waters. But it's the excitement and adventure that make it all worthwhile. If you never make the attempt, you may never know the depth of despair but neither will you experience the exhilaration of success.

Decide to live life to the fullest.
You may be three feet from gold.

– Napoleon Hill

BUILD WEALTH TAX FREE

Turbo-Charge Your IRA

The idea behind the IRA (Individual Retirement Account) when it was established back in 1974 was to help the average person put away some "extra" money to supplement their pension and Social Security income. Social Security was never intended to cover a person's entire retirement needs and not every company offered attractive retirement plans. The goal was to encourage Americans to save a little nest egg.

By now, most of us are well aware that that little nest egg won't go very far. Pension plans gave way to 401(k) plans, Social Security has been gutted by inflation, political game-playing and the economic downturn.

None of us wants to retire into a lower standard of living. Yet millions of Americans are facing that reality every day. 35% of Americans over the age of 65 rely almost entirely on Social Security alone. And 56% of retirees believe that the government will eventually cut their Social Security benefits. I don't think that is a position that any of us wants to be in.

Social Security was never intended to be the sole financial support of retirees. It was meant to supplement pensions, savings and other investments. IRAs were instituted to help people save for retirement. Yet approximately half of all American workers have less than $2,000 saved for retirement!

And the era of a cushy retirement plan went out when IRAs came in. Businesses phased out pension plans and phased in 401(k) and other retirement plans that relied on employee contributions. Even if you contributed steadily to your company's pension plan, you might have come up with the short end of the stick; the number of pensions at risk inside failing companies more than tripled during the recession with more pension plans, including city, county and state government plans, ready to topple.

IRA CONTRIBUTIONS WON'T GET YOU THERE

You can contribute up to $5,000 per year into an IRA if you are under 50 years of age; up to $6,000 per year if you are over 50, up to the total of your taxable compensation. That means that if you only had $4,000 of taxable income, you can only contribute $4,000 to your IRA.

The rules are slightly different for a Roth IRA; the amount you can contribute depends on your income. You can make the full contribution of $5,000 if your modified adjusted gross income is less than $105,000 ($167,000 if married filing jointly). You may be able to make a smaller contribution if you earn up to $120,000 ($177,000 if married, filing jointly).

So, if you are 50 years old, single and earning less than $105,000 per year and looking to retire at age 65, you can contribute $6,000 a year for the next 15 years or what amounts to about $90,000. At 9% interest compounded daily, that amount would grow to $215,000. It would take you 15 years to put aside what you earn in less than three or four years now. How long do you think that money will last? And we didn't factor in inflation. No wonder 24% of U.S. workers admit that they have postponed their planned retirement age at least once during the past year.

Obviously, you need to make the money in your IRA work and work hard.

THE POWER OF COMPOUND INTEREST

"Compound interest is the most powerful force on Earth."

–Albert Einstein

How powerful is compound interest? Let's take a look at $100,000 compounded over 30 years at 9% interest. The only thing that is going to change in this equation is the rate that the interest is compounded: Yearly, Weekly, Monthly and Daily.

$100,000   at 9%

Compounded Yearly (once a year):	1,326,767.85
Compounded Monthly (12x a year):	1,473,057.61
Compounded Weekly (52x a year):	1,484,504.52
Compounded Daily (365 x a year):	1,487,478.02

The difference between compounding daily and compounding yearly is almost $150,000. That's better than a sharp stick in your eye. Not excited? How about this: $500,000 at 9 compounded yearly for 30 years is $6,633,839.23. Compounded daily, that same $500,000 is 7,437,390.12. Almost a million dollars more.

So compounding is a powerful force indeed. But what happens when you use the power of compounding in a tax-free account? Take a look at the chart on the next page.

Initial Deposit	$10,000	
Interest Rate	9%	
Federal and State Tax	36%	
Inflation	0 (for simplicity's sake)	
Year	Value with **Tax Free** Compounding	Value with **Taxed** Compounding
1 Year Value	10,941.17	10,602.72
2 Year Value	11,972.17	11,241.76
3 Year Value	13,099.64	11,919.32
4 Year Value	14,333.29	12,637.71
5 Year Value	15,683.12	13,399.41
10 Year Value	24,596.03	17,954.41
15 Year Value	38,574.26	24,057.84
20 Year Value	**60,496.47**	**32,236.07**
30 Year Value	148,797.32	57,877.95
40 Year Value	**365,98234**	**103,916.42**

The difference over twenty years is obvious; the difference over 30 or 40 years is nothing short of stunning.

It's extremely powerful to grow your money either tax-free or tax-deferred. But for some of us (indeed, most of us!) compound interest alone isn't going to get us where we need to be.

So how can we make it even better?

Strap Yourselves In

Self-directed IRA investors can leverage the power of tax-free investing in a way that most Americans have never heard or even thought of. You can use a Limited Liability Company in conjunction with your self-directed IRA to create the earnings you need to truly fund your retirement. You won't have to worry about Social Security going broke or delay your plans for retirement. I am about to show you just one way to turbo-charge your Self Directed IRA that will change the way you view retirement accounts forever.

How does the Limited Liability Company Structured IRA work? The account holder directs his IRA custodian to invest into a limited liability company that the account owner manages himself. The account owner can then execute transactions on the LLC level without the involvement of the IRA custodian, thus reducing fees and eliminating custodian transactional fees and delays. The profits of the LLC pass through to the IRA with nearly identical tax favorable treatment.

Does it sound too good to be true? I thought so too, until I read up on a 1996 IRS case, Swanson vs. Commissioner of Internal Revenue. James Swanson had a company that manufactured tools. He established a second company as a sales company. Mr. Swanson was the officer and manager of both companies, but he was not the owner of the sales company, he was the Director of the company. The sales company was *owned* by Mr. Swanson's self-directed IRA. The manufacturing company paid a commission to the sales company for every tool sale they made. Mr. Swanson's IRA received about 200,000 a year each year because the commissions that were paid to the sales company "flowed" through to the IRA.

The IRS sued him and after a four year battle, the court ruled that this structure was legal. Mr. Swanson won the case and was awarded damages, including his lawyers' fees.

Think about how you could use this structure. Are you a professional? Do you lease equipment? Do you lease offices? Could you set up a separate company to coordinate and/or service your main company's business?

For instance, if you have rental houses, could you have a separate property management company that you paid to manage those houses? If you ran a retail store or even a service business, could your IRA own an LLC that does marketing and advertising?

Think of what type of support company your primary business could legitimately use. Set up your second company, structuring it carefully and with the help of a competent legal professional and have it owned either partially or completely by your IRA.

This accomplishes two things: First, it reduces your income by the amount you pay in rent and second, the money can ultimately flow through into your IRA.

Self Directed IRAs

What can your Self-Directed IRA invest in? There are literally hundreds of investment opportunities that allow you to have control of your investments.

Of course you can invest in traditional assets such as Stocks, Bonds and Mutual Funds.

But a Self-Directed IRA can do so much more. Here are just a few other options:

Invest in Real Estate and Real Estate Paper

Residential Property	Commercial Property
Developed Land	Undeveloped Land
Foreclosures	Rehabs/Flips
Mobile Homes	Tax Liens/Tax Deeds
Tax Lien	Tax Deed
Mortgages/Deeds of Trust	

Invest in Other Types of Paper:

Promissory Notes	Secured Notes	Unsecured Notes
Car Paper	Commercial Paper	

Invest in various entities such as Private Placements, Limited Liability Companies and Limited Partnerships. Think of the Swanson case and the amount of money his second company poured into his self-directed IRA.

Your Self-Directed IRA can also invest in:

Structured Settlements	Factoring
Accounts Receivable	Equipment Leasing
Foreign Currency Exchange (FOREX)	

Don't limit yourself or your thinking and you will find that the options for your Self-Directed IRA are just about unlimited.

What can't you invest in?

There are a few IRA investments the IRS prohibits, including:

| Artworks | Rugs | Antiques | Metals |
| Gems | Stamps | Coins | Certain Collectibles |

The best investment on earth is earth. Buying land is the road to wealth and your IRA is the vehicle you should use to travel down that road. In the long run, putting land in your IRA will get you further down the road faster than you thought possible.

Why is that? Why do you think land is probably going to be the key to your retirement and your wealth?

Because the availability of land diminishes all the time. As more and more people are born and mature into potential landowners, there will be less and less land available to buy.

How can knowing that help you? I am going to show you how to get involved in land investing by using your IRA. They are not making any more land, are they? No, it is getting used up very rapidly.

Land is the American Dream. Land is being developed faster than ever as the population explodes. Undeveloped land is just one method that can provide cash flow monthly into your IRA just like rental property but without the headaches. I plan to open up some new options for you, show you six turnkey investment secrets and perhaps introduce you to some investment strategies you have never before considered. You will see that not all of my strategies involve real estate however all of these strategies involve using your IRA to build wealth exponentially.

I will teach you how to buy real estate and other investments in your IRA, how to use turnkey systems to create wealth tax-free and how to reinvest that income to work even harder for you.

I have been investing for over 20 years, and the last six or seven have been almost perfect. But, in the past, I made my share of mistakes. I bought many parcels of land, made some good choices and some bad ones. I have investigated various wealth building strategies from the ground up, I have watched markets come and go – real estate, the dotcom boom and bust, and everything in between. From those experiences, I have compiled the secrets to building wealth in your IRA. I will share these secrets with you so you do not make the same mistakes. You will move directly towards success.

Risk versus Reward for Your IRA

Let's talk about risk versus reward. We all agree that your IRA is for long-term investments. That does not mean that you should ignore the returns you are getting in your IRA.

Stock Market

You know about the stock market. You have seen stock markets crash. You have seen stocks take dips. I can tell you that the risk of stocks and mutual funds is unnecessary. At any age, there is no reason to have to take that risk, lose 50 percent of your money in mutual funds and wait forever for the funds to go back up. It happens all the time. I bought many mutual funds over the past 20 years. Some I have made money on, and some I have not. The point is that I rarely got ahead. Whenever I got behind, I was stuck for long periods of time and could not recover enough to break even. I have stopped wasting my time and money.

Rental Properties

Let's take a look at the risk/reward for rental properties in your IRA. Rental properties present some high return opportunities but they also have the downside of big headaches!

There is nothing wrong with buying rental properties with your IRA. There is nothing wrong with buying commercial real estate. But, there is a smart way to do it and a run-yourself-ragged way to do it. We love real estate here at Poggi Wealth Institute, but we also know that you don't get ahead by scouting properties, negotiating deals, fixing up and then either selling or renting properties one at a time. We like to get the most return for our dollars *and time*. Too many investors don't factor in the time they spend on their investments. That factor infringes on your lifestyle and your freedom.

Here is a summary of typical risk/reward:

Stocks: High risk, no control, huge downside.

Mutual Funds: Can be moderate risk, huge downside.

Bonds: Low risk, very low return, low upside.

CDs: Low risk, very low return, low upside.

Cash: Lose some money to inflation, no growth.

Land/Properties: Low risk, high return, and can cash flow if you follow a set of strict rules!

Real Estate or Mutual Fund?
Which Earns the Most?

Now let's talk about mutual funds for a second. If you were to invest $10,000 in a mutual fund or $10,000 in a piece of land, which has the greater chance of decreasing in value?

Let's say you have a choice to invest $10,000 in a piece of land. The chances of your land dropping in value, going from $10,000 to $5,000, are very unlikely. Probably the worst case scenario is it would stay the same.

But in a mutual fund, could the value go from $10,000 to $5,000? Absolutely. And then to recover, to go from $5,000 back to break even, then back to 50 percent higher is a process that could take a lifetime. It is ridiculous!

As a stockbroker, I bought many mutual funds for myself and my family -- I thought I was doing the safe thing -- until the stock market took a dive and everyone lost money. I felt sick over it. I thought to myself, "Why do I need to buy investments that have the potential to drop in half?" There is no reason for that. So I stopped gambling on mutual funds. The same goes for stocks.

If you do not already have an IRA, you should open one immediately! That is where you should be spending your time, focusing on your investments in your IRA. Investments within your IRA should get you to your magic number for retirement faster than investing outside your IRA. The IRA is a tool for you to be able to invest in real estate and recognize gains or income in the IRA without having to pay taxes immediately. Many people do not realize that they can and should purchase real estate and other high-return investments in their IRA.

Most people invest in real estate outside of their IRA and get hammered by taxes on their rental income and on the profit from the sale of their property. On the other hand, they hold cash, CDs and mutual funds in their IRAs when these rarely need a tax shelter because they have low returns.

If you invest using your IRA, the income and growth can be tax-free, providing you with additional funds to purchase more vacant lots, more houses, or invest in any of our six strategies. If you do not have enough money in your IRA, you can leverage your IRA and borrow money from an individual or lender to purchase any type of property using a non-recourse loan.

Dynasty Roth IRAs
You Don't Need a Crystal Ball

What does the future hold? It would be a huge benefit to have a crystal ball to see what is going to happen in the future, what's going to happen with taxes, health costs, the market. No matter how old we are, all of us should be thinking about our future and retirement. I'm just going to mention three or four items briefly about the future, and they are living longer, obviously, health costs, market risk and taxes. All these play a big part in what we're trying to do with our financial planning, especially tax-free planning.

Many people have been warning against the ramifications of the high U.S. debt level for a long time. Now even the Comptroller of the United States, David Walker, is sounding the alarm. The Comptroller recently warned that, "If the country continues on its current fiscal past, it would gradually erode and have an adverse impact on the economy and the nation's standard of living over time and America's national security." He went on to say that, "The U.S. taxes would have to double to account for the Bush deficit in 2004." Recently, a hearing took place at the Capitol regarding the current economic situation, and the U.S. economy is in a serious attempt to restrain spending. Now, Walker conveyed that since 2000, the net Social Security commitment and other fiscal obligations in the United States have surged from $20 trillion to $50 trillion, which is quadruple this country's total economic output. He noted that rising healthcare cost was the greatest contributor to the increase. To put it in perspective, he said, "To balance the budget by the year 2040, the government would require either action as big as reducing total spending by 60% or increasing federal taxes almost two times its current level."

This is saying to you that in the future, and it doesn't have to be 2040, we can see it coming right now, that three things can happen with taxes: They can stay the same, they can go up or they can go down. Two of them are in our favor. If they stay the same or go up, a conversion to a Roth IRA is very important for everybody to beat the system just in taxes alone. It's unbelievable what it's going to cost you for health costs in the future. We know what it's costing Ford and General Motors. They're bankrupt because they can't afford to pay all the benefits and the government probably will not be able to pay all its benefits. They're just going to reduce the benefits and raise taxes to accommodate this level because people are living a lot longer. Nobody ever expected that.

Just to give you an idea about how longevity plays into your long-term planning, if you're a male, age 65, you have a 50% chance of living to 85 and a 25% chance of living to 92. If you're a female at age 65, you have a 50% chance of making it to 88 and a 25% chance to make it to 94. If you are a couple, both age 65, there's a 50% chance that one of you will make it to 92 and a 25% change that one of you will make it to 97. Well, living longer is great, but you have to plan for that longer life span. At age 65, you can see that we're talking about a life expectancy of another 20 to 30 years. Just think what's happened with inflation in the last 20 or 30 years and how you can protect your dollar, either through asset protection or good growth and we're talking about growth being tax-free. In addition to that, just to give you an average, if you were 65 today, your life expectancy is 21 years.

How do you make sure you have money to last you all of your life? One of the best ways is to have your money in a Roth plan. You can convert not only traditional IRAs but 401(k)s, profit-sharing plans, 403(b) plans, the SEPs, and SIMPLEs to a Roth IRA. Now, when you do convert, you must pay income tax on the contributions that were made earlier to the typical IRA or 401(k) plan that was deducted against your income. Taxes must be paid on the investment gains that you made. So you will have to pay taxes on the entire account, contributions and gains. It could be worthwhile converting if you expect your tax rate to be the same or higher when your money is ultimately withdrawn. A conversion will result in a tax bill when you move funds into the Roth IRA, but investors could avoid future federal taxes on any subsequent Roth IRA earnings and withdrawals. Also, you don't have to convert the entire amount if you don't want to.

Do You Qualify for a Roth IRA?

You may not qualify for a Roth IRA. One reason may be because you make too much money. That would be somebody who is single, basically making more than $110,000 a year or someone who is married, filing jointly and making over $160,000. Generally speaking, you are not eligible for a Roth IRA.

The second qualifier is that if you already have an existing 401(k) or an IRA, a traditional IRA, or a SEP or SIMPLE, and you want to covert that today to a Roth IRA, you have to have an adjusted gross income, whether you're single or married, of less than $100,000. So when I go around the country speaking, a lot of people say, "Gee, I can't have a Roth IRA or I can't convert because I make too much money." The answer to solving that problem is to get your income down so that you can convert and have a Roth IRA; and obviously, when you do the conversion, you're going to have a tax bill due.

As I always say, it is better to pay tax on the seed than the crop, or it's better to pay tax on $10,000 rather than the $100,000 you could have after you grow your IRA account. So for that reason alone, it's imperative that you take traditional IRA money or 401(k) money, and in almost all cases, there might be an exception or two why you would not do it, but in general, it's to your advantage in my opinion, to convert and pay the tax now. Pay the tax on the seed, not the crop.

Now, once you get that conversion and you get the money in the account, a lot of good things can happen. A Roth IRA is the best investment that you can ever make. It's tax-free, you never, ever pay any federal income tax and it's a form of asset protection. Nobody can get at it except the IRS or your spouse.

Case Studies

I'm going to show you some examples of what that really means. The first two examples I'll give you use a one-time, $4,000 investment in a Roth IRA today and we're going to use a child, age 10 in our example. I'm going to use an 8% return and a 10% return on that $4,000. Then I'll show you the numbers using $20,000 and having an 8% and a 10% return on that money over the life expectancy over that 10 year old child.

For the last example, I'll use a husband and wife who are 40 and 35 with a 15 year old son. I'll show you the power of this IRA account that has been converted to a Roth IRA by paying a little bit of tax upfront, making one $4,000 investment in 2007 and having it inside of a Roth IRA account, earning only 8% over the life expectancy of that child which would be 81.

One of the benefits of a Roth IRA is that unlike traditional IRAs and other retirement accounts, you're not required to take money out of the account starting at age 70½. In this account, if you don't need the money, you can let it grow. If you do need the money, you can take it out and spend it and it's tax-free. Now, just one investment of $4,000, with no additional contributions, earning 8%, would grow to over a million dollars over the life expectancy of that 10 year old child. Even at age 65, that account's worth about $300,000. At age 60, it's worth about $200,000.

Let's just kick it up now and say instead of earning 8% in that account, we were able to earn 10%. Well, that $4,000 one-time investment would be worth not $1 million, but $3,818,000. At age 60, the account would be approximately$500,000 and at age 65, it would be $831,000. So one $4,000 investment put away earning 8% or 10% is worth between $1 million and almost $4 million, and the only place that can happen is inside that tax-free account. I use that to show you the power of what we're talking about: Compounding interest tax-free over time.

I am a huge fan of the Roth 401(k). If you start this year, you can, if you're under 50 years old, contribute $15,500 and if you're over 50, you could contribute $20,500. So just think that no matter what your income level is, you could put in $15,500 in for you, your spouse and your child, if you have a child. Now, what we're going to do is show you what this power can do with just one $15,500 investment and also putting in a contribution of your Roth IRA of approximately $4,500. That adds up to $20,000.

Now, if you started that account for your son or daughter at age 10, with $20,000, at 8%, that account will be worth over $5 million at full life expectancy. At age 60, that account will be worth $1 million. At 65, if the person didn't want to spend the money and take it out, there's $1½ million to spend over their life expectancy and still continue to earn money. Again, as I said, this is only earning 8% or 10% on your money.

The last piece of this, that $20,000 one-time investment earning 10%, from age 10, at 60, that'll be worth $2½ million; at 65, it'll be worth $4 million, and over the full life expectancy, at 81, that would be worth $19 million. That's earning 10% over a 30- or 40-year period. Now, some people say you can earn that and some people say you can't. I just know this: Statistically over a long period of time of 30, 40 or 50 years, many mutual funds and even the Standard and Poor's Index have averaged between 10% and

12%. We can't predict the future but in the last 40 or 50 years, that's what we've done. So these are reasonable numbers that can grow tax-free and not pay any tax on them and have asset protection.

Now that was for somebody young, ten years old. Let's work an example with people who are a little older.

Take a husband and wife who are 40 and 35 respectively with a 15 year old son. We make the same one-time $20,000 contribution today, just for the husband, not in all three accounts. We start in 2012. According to our life expectancy charts, the husband would die in 2052 and his account, at that stage, would be worth $470,000. That account would transfer to his wife, no estate taxes; it is a spousal roll. It would be her IRA account, and she would name her son as the beneficiary. In this scenario, she doesn't need the money. She continues to let that grow, and she dies in the year 2068. At that point, the account would be worth $1½ million. She leaves it to her son and it is estate tax-free at this level. He then would take it out at this stage; it's mandatory. When somebody is a beneficiary of an IRA account or retirement account and is not the original IRA holder's spouse, you have to take it out and take the minimum required distribution. You can take it all out at once but if you do so, you lose the ability of the stretch out that dynasty account. That means that the ability of that account to grow tax-free for the rest of your life and your children's life basically. So at 2068, that $1½ million account is inherited by the son and he takes it out over his life expectancy, which would be about 16 more years. As he draws it out yearly, part of it is still growing tax-free. The son will have taken out of that account $2.8 million tax-free and that was from a $20,000 one- time investment earning 8% and letting it grow.

There's a tremendous benefit in that and it's all because you took a little bit of time and money and planned according to the tax laws available to you today.

What happens if that $20,000, in the same situation, earned a 10% return instead of earning 8%? When the husband died, the account would be worth $1 million; it goes to his spouse tax-free. She allows it to grow and leaves it to her son. She didn't take any money out and she wasn't required to. Between the husband and wife, they let the account grow tax-free, only at 10%, and this time, when the wife passes away, that account is worth over $4 million.

Leaving it to the son, again, with those 16 years to take that money out tax-free, he will take out *$9½ million* for a one-time $20,000 investment.

Can you see the power of investing money tax-free?

Now, I've just used a $4,000 or a $20,000 one-time investment. What if you took that $5,000 or $20,000 and turned it into $30,000, $40,000, $50,000, $60,000, $80,000 or $100,000 doing some real estate deals or doing some of the creative strategies that we teach? If you put that money to work, it could be 4 or 5 times what I've told you; and you don't even have to look at 10% returns. You can look at returns of 6%, 7%, 8%. What if you started with $40,000? It's very easy to do that using the strategies that we have in place.

Now that you know what's happening in the future as far as life expectancy and health costs, the market and all the other factors that come into play, you can see the power of compounding your money tax-free. The government gave us the biggest prize in the world. They said, "In 2010, no matter what your income is, you can convert all your money, whether you have a Roth IRA or not; and when you do that, you have two years to pay the tax." In essence, you could split your tax bill for converting to a Roth IRA, paying half in 2010 and half in 2011.

Now, 2010 has come and gone but you can still limit your taxes if you convert your traditional IRA or 401(k) to a Roth. If you are at the 35% federal tax level, and you do some planning, which we're talking about now, you can reduce your taxable income in the year that you're going to make your conversion and your tax rate might be lower. A second strategy, if you live in a state that has state income tax and you're thinking about moving to a state like Florida or Texas or Nevada that has no state income tax, you can convert to a Roth IRA after you move, and save yourself anywhere from approximately 10% and maybe even 12% on state income taxes. So you can see that we should start today to plan how to maximize your account so that you get more money into the account, so that you'll pay less tax, so that you'll have it asset protected and you'll have it so that you'll never have to take any money out of the account unless you want to.

Now, somebody may ask, "Why do I need to convert?" Well, one of the things I told you is that if you know what the tax rate is today or what it's going to be, do you think the tax rates are going to be higher in the future? Face it; you're going to have to pay more money in the future. Now, you and I know that the deficit spending that we've got now with the Democrats in Congress, it's a good likelihood that the tax rates will go up; either the capital gains or the marginal tax rates will go higher and there's a good chance that'll happen. Also, by the conversion, you can reduce your future tax basis. If you're making too much money, it's going to reduce your Social Security benefits. So if you get this money in a tax-free account that you don't have to take it out, it wouldn't cause you to make more money, so that you can maximize your Social Security benefits. The income from your traditional IRA that you are required to take out after age 70½ might put you in a higher tax bracket. With the Roth IRA, you do not have to take the money out at 70½.

Another thing about this is that if you are the beneficiary of an IRA account or 401(k) plan and you do receive it, you can disown it and pass it on to a contingent beneficiary such as your children or grandchildren. So again, you can have a longer time span to grow that account tax-free and, if you don't need or use the money, you can leave an account or an estate to your children or your grandchildren that would grow tax-free. So that's why I used the example. If you were to leave your child or grandchild, age 10, $5,000 or $20,000 in a tax-free account and let it grow, that'll be worth anywhere from $2 million to $4 million when they turn 65 or 70 years old. Put it in some investments, and as I said before, if you're able to take that $5,000, $10,000 or $20,000 and grow it before you need to get conservative with the money; You can multiply it and make it worth $5 million or $10 million. Again, that account is your account. Anytime you want that money, you can take it out. You can spend it and it's not like you don't have ability to get control of it because all you need with a tax-free account is to have the account open for five years and you have to be 59½, and then you can take a qualified distribution; it's tax-free to you and your spouse and your children.

Now, what else could you do better than that? Now, why would you want to keep your money in a traditional IRA? I'm a big proponent of consolidating your money and getting as much money as you can in your Roth IRA or a 401(k) Roth. I like that because basically the maximum amount of money you can put into your Roth right now is $5,000 or $6,000 if you're over 50. So again, if you have the ability to direct your IRA, leverage it and make a lot of money using maybe a lease option or an option on something or buying a discounted bond or note, you might multiply that substantially.

What if you had ability to put even more money in that account? Would you do it? Of course you would and one of the things now with the Roth 401(k) is that if you open up a 401(k) with our help, and if you're married and you had a child, you're able to put $15,000, $15,000 and $15,000, $45,000 in one year plus another $15,000 basically. So you're talking $60,000 into a Roth IRA every year, up to that level. If you're over 50, then you can put not only $15,000, you could put $20,000 in.

Why do you want more money in that account tax-free? As I told you, first of all, it is asset protected. The second thing is it gives you the ability to handle bigger deals. The more options that you have to make your investments, the better off you are. Many people say, "Gee, I need more money for my deals." You can, under certain circumstances properly structured, have one account that invests your money for you and your spouse and your children together, proportionately, and you can be your own private bank. You could start loaning that money out at 10%, 15% a year if you wanted to.

Some Now, Some Later

You can have some investments that you make money on right away. You can have some money investments that you know will pay off in four or five years. For example, if your city is growing, the real estate that is now on the outskirts of town is going to become more valuable. You might make some investments that you don't need the income right away but you know it's going to be there four or five years from now. So having more money gives you more options. It gives you control and it is easy to manage. It helps your family basically in managing money by saying, "Here's our Poggi IRA Bank; and we've got a million dollars in this account and we're going to make an investment here and we're going to make an investment here, and here's the returns at the end of the year because we have a little partnership there."

Where's the Break-Even on Converting?

I have had several people ask me, "Considering the statistics of how long people are expected to live, depending on the age that you are today when you make the conversion, does Equity Trust have or is there any place to go to get a mathematical formula for what kind of a return you would have to make each year in order for us to break even and then to see when we start coming out ahead?"

Well, that's a simple answer. You don't even have to do a calculation on that. The real question here is "Am I better off by taking $100,000 and paying the tax on it and then taking that money and reinvesting it and then not having to pay any tax; or postpone paying the tax and let the $100,000 grow forever and then pay the tax when I take it out?" Well, there's absolutely no difference if the tax rate stays the same as it is today and when you take it out. Therefore, it doesn't matter. You don't lose any benefit except the one thing is that you are able to pay the federal income tax today out of your own pocket and not out of your IRA account. So if you took a distribution of $100,000, you're going to have $65,000 to invest and you're going to pay $35,000 in tax. Right now, if you do that investment, you'll have $100,000 to roll tax-free; and you can pay the $35,000 of tax that's due on that out of your own pocket, no matter how you do it.

Now that's if the tax rate stays the same. I have given you enough statistics that show the high probability of tax rates going up in the future. I guarantee you, next year your taxes are going up against this year. Using what we teach, you can avoid paying the full 35% if that is your current tax bracket. If you can reduce your taxable income, bring your tax rate down to maybe 15% or 20%, then it's a tremendous benefit for you to convert. I've only used 35% because that's a federal income tax level. Now, what happens if you live in a state like New York where you're paying another 10% or 12% and I said, "Gee, in 2012, are you going to live in Florida for a year?" If you had a million dollar account and you had to pay 10% or 12% tax, you just saved yourself $120,000 by moving to Florida for a year or another state that doesn't have a state income tax. Go live with your children in another state. Does that sound far-fetched? Why do you think so many people have left California and gone to Arizona or Nevada or Texas? Those states have lower taxes and California state taxes are so high. The only way you can lose in this deal is if the tax rates go down later on, and the chances of that happening are very slim.

Why Doesn't My Financial Planner Know About This?

There are really only a few financial planners who understand the techniques that our company uses. There are no particular financial planners that we know that have resources that are particularly adept at following the investor methods that we teach. They all came from the same school, and they're either insurance agents or stock brokers or people that are a combination of both; and they're interested in gathering money and selling you a product. That's how they make their money.

They're not there to hold your hand and educate you like I am. I can show you some ideas and you can make a lot of money by listening to some of my techniques and trying them because whenever I have a seminar or do anything, I guarantee you there are attorneys there. There are CPAs there, and they're all saying, "I didn't know you could do all this stuff." And they still don't know. You can't educate those people. It would take you forever. You go ask your banker, your CPA or financial planner, if you can take your IRA money or 401(k) money and invest it in real estate, they'll say, "You can't do that. You can't touch your IRA money." They'll tell you that you can't buy a tax lien, which is about the safest thing in the world right now because you've got tremendous protection on a tax lien. Tax liens are paying anywhere from the 9% to 30% return on your money, depending on where you buy it. When you buy a tax lien, you get the first mortgage on a house, you're headed to the bank; and unless you bought a toxic dump, there is hardly any way you can lose. But most advisors don't know you can buy tax liens with your IRA.

Are those financial planners guaranteeing you or paying you 10% to 15%, 20% on your money? No way. The biggest problem is that the mutual fund industry really doesn't understand the impact of the dynasty IRA, of this money compounding tax-free for all those of years. For many years, I was telling you about the Roth 401(k) and I have preached forever about the Roth being the most powerful method of money growing tax-free. We just teach and educate everyone to help investors make money because our business is built on referral business. Seventy percent of our customers come to us because someone they know had good results with us.

We help you make money. Weren't those case study numbers dynamic that I showed you? One $5,000 investment turns into $4 million or $5 million or a $20,000 investment grows to $9 million, with an 8% to 10% return. Those aren't pie-in-the-sky rates of return. You go look at any decent mutual fund over a 30-, 40-year-period, look at the S&P what it's done. S&P has averaged 12% since 1925, and we're talking 8% to 10%. It's the power of time and tax-free compounding. That's why we call it a Dynasty IRA. Just think if you put $20,000 in a Roth 401(k) today, you did a lease option on that or you bought a piece of property that you took the $20,000 and made $40,000; and then next year, you start investing money at 8% to 10%. Now you've got $40,000. All those numbers I talked about, just double them. Now I'm sure that you have more money than $20,000, so we're not talking about all the money that you have or your personal money, your personal assets, your stocks and bonds that you own. We're talking about some of it, and guess what? When you see how much money you're making tax-free, you're going to try to get as much money in those accounts for yourself and your family and your children and your grandchildren, even if you split the account up a little bit. Suppose you had a million dollars. I said, "I'm going to keep $800,000 and give $50,000 to my four grandchildren or $20,000 to my four grandchildren or $10,000." And what are you giving them, a Christmas account that they can spend the money at the end of the year when Christmas comes? You're giving them an account that will grow tax-free for the rest of their lives no matter how much money they make and nobody can come after that and sue them and take their account. You're giving them security and financial freedom.

Many people ask me about their parents. For example: let's say my mom is 70½, and she is taking her withdrawals at this point and has about $500,000 in her IRA. Does it make any sense for her to open a Roth or not and take any, kind of tax hit? Let's say that her income level right now is just under $50,000, or $60,000. My mother is in good health, so her life expectancy right now is probably going to be about 20 years. Wouldn't it be nice to know that if you have a good income and you said, "Mom, you've got $500,000 in this account, and let's structure this deal so that we pay that tax over two or three years." So we take $150,000 each year. Using a 30% tax rate, she'd have to pay about $45,000 in taxes. You say, "Mom, I'm going to pay that for you so you don't have to worry about it." So the first year you pay $45,000, the second year $45,000 and the third year you pay $45,000.

Now she has $500,000 that she can take out and not have to pay any income tax on that. Even if her income tax rate is low, it's going to be a big benefit to her by saying, "You don't pay any income tax." It can grow tax-free, she can take it out tax-free. But she's *not required* to take money out. Now, guess what happens? If you are the beneficiary of that $500,000, you get a tax-free account. Or your spouse, and if you get it and you say, "I only want $200,000 in my name and I want $300,000 on my four kids." That's $75,000 a piece. You've got an account that grows tax-free for the rest of their lives. That's what she wants: Long-term wealth for her family.

Using a Self-Directed IRA to Invest in a Business

Can you invest your Self-Directed IRA money into a partnership in a business? You can't in any way, shape or form have anything to do with the profitability of a partnership or the company that you're investing in. It's ironic, but I can go buy a piece of property with that money, improve the property and still reap the rewards.

So in essence, I can do it if I do it in real estate; but if I venture into a business, I can't have anything to do with making a profit. The money has to be invested on its own and it has to earn interest or income based on the merits of the company you invest in. But you can't have any control as to whether or not that company makes money.

Here's the difference in the dilemma. Number one, when you make an investment in land or real estate, it is what we call a "passive investment." The land goes up in value and you make money. If you buy a building, and it goes up, you make money. But if, as the IRS has said, you are a fiduciary, you cannot do a prohibited transaction or invest with a disqualified person. A fiduciary is a disqualified person, so now if you are going to work for this company and you could be a director and not work for the company. You can hire people to work for you and run the business and reap the rewards. I believe owning a business in your IRA is a great thing to do. It just has to be structured properly and you have to be convinced that the way to do it legally is a good way to do it. You're going to make a lot more money and maybe there's another way for you to get into another business, that you use that business to make your money and the other one to make money tax-free inside your IRA account.

So yes, you can invest in a business. I have many people that have and are very happy making a lot of money doing this. But you really need to understand how to structure it properly and take the time to do it right.

Asset protection is very, very important. There's a possibility that if you properly structure your investments, that your state taxes will be reduced or eliminated completely so that you have an account that grows tax-free. You can take it out and spend it tax-free and you have no transfer tax or state tax to pay. You don't have to worry about what the federal taxes are and who's going to come after your account because it's all taken care of.

You are at the beginning of this now, the whole concept that we have to start planning ahead because that affects everybody no matter how much money you make. You need to prepare to plan ahead for how you're going to pay the taxes, if and how you are going to reduce your income when you convert to a Roth plan, what investments you're going to do and how big the accounts will be when you get them there.

I think that the subject of getting this tax-free account is so important, that there are so many different possibilities for your money, your parents' money, you getting tax-free income today and never paying any tax; and the most important thing is so many people are going to have 401(k) plans that, in the next three or four or five years will be coming due and you're going to have to do something about it; and you'll have the ability to convert that to a Roth IRA.

Turnkey Investment Secret Strategy #1

LOW PRICED LOTS

Turnkey Investment Secret Strategy Number 1 is investing in low-priced lots. Now that doesn't sound like it would be too complicated, does it? And it's not, providing you know what to look for, know where to look for it, what to pay for it and how to sell it at a profit. I'm about to show you all those things. I am sure, that after reading this chapter, you'll become as big a fan of investment lots as I am.

What You Will Learn from this Chapter

This chapter will teach you how to use your IRA to buy vacant lots in established, fast-growing resort communities that have been around for years.

We teach investors a proven system to make huge returns from vacant lots which will provide cash flow tax-free into an IRA. We specialize in resort communities because we have learned that they are safer and appreciate faster. We do not buy in Florida, California or in the middle of nowhere in Tennessee. We do not buy in those places because the value of the land is over-inflated. I am going to teach you the best way to make money in land and avoid the pitfalls.

We only focus on resort communities that have amenities – for example, a golf course or marina. This is important because when you want to sell, you have a better chance of selling a lot in a community with several amenities. If you do not have <u>amenities</u> and <u>growth</u> and <u>price</u>, you do not win this game.

Again, you absolutely need three things: Low purchase price, variety of amenities, and explosive growth potential. We will show you how to locate these areas.

The Key to My Company's Success

Why have I chosen Vacant Lots as my #1 Turnkey Investment Strategy? My background has been in real estate for over 20 years and the stock market for over 15 years. I owned a stock brokerage firm in Chicago and learned a lot about mutual funds and stocks. I made and lost millions in the stock market and in mutual funds. You may have had experiences with the stock market as well. I have already discussed the risk/reward of stocks, bonds, mutual funds, land, houses, etc. earlier in this book. Believe me, those were hard learned lessons.

I speak all over the country on how to build wealth with land in your IRA tax-free. That is my specialty. I have made enough mistakes and spent enough money the WRONG WAY to tell you what NOT to do. That is why I consider myself an expert. I have made mistakes and, as a result, have perfected a system. Because I have completed hundreds of land deals, I can teach you the secret way to build wealth with land in your IRA which can be duplicated over and over again.

One of my companies, Build Wealth With Land, is a leading provider of pre-platted buildable home sites for investors and builders. We are not a real estate office that has listings; we are a bulk land company that helps people fill their portfolios or IRAs with quarter acre buildable vacant lots in resort communities.

We do not deal in large parcels of land. We do not buy from a builder and split the land into lots. We are buying individual lots from individual people and selling those lots to investors and builders. We do not buy pre-construction lots from a developer. That is not the best way to buy land.

The Potential Value of Low Priced Lots

Similar to mutual funds, land value can drop in half, if it is a high-priced lot. A $100,000 lot can drop to $80,000 or $70,000 pretty easily. I am not saying that land value never goes down; I am saying that low-priced lots, below $20,000, rarely drop in value. Land value for a low-priced lot either stays the same or goes up because the value is not artificially inflated.

A $100,000 lot can fluctuate. In Florida, land fell from $100,000 to $50,000 in several months. That is one reason why I strongly suggest that you do not buy high-priced lots.

Low-priced lots are the secret, and those lots have low risk. For example, a $5,000 lot is not going to drop to $2,000. It just does not happen. They stay the same or go up. That is your downside risk.

Always measure your downside risk. You cannot make an investment and say, "What am I going to earn?" How about, "What am I going to lose?" That is important because making money is one thing, but *not losing money* is another. Many of us are guilty of buying something because of greed or excitement, but we did not anticipate a downside. So if you buy something too high and it goes down, you lose a portion of your investment all because you were excited and motivated for the wrong reasons. You absolutely have got to measure your downside risk. Downside is just as important as upside.

What Is the Best Investment: Land or Houses?

You might be wondering, "Why should I invest in land in addition to houses?" I will tell you why. Houses can be a real headache compared to empty lots. I have houses that I purchase on a monthly basis. I use a system to fix them up and sell them wholesale. By doing this, I do not get problem phone calls or "headache calls" all the time, as you might from rental properties.

I do not get any phone calls on my vacant lots. I have no tenants, no aggravation, nothing to think about, no repairs, and nothing to worry about. So vacant land is a much easier investment. I believe that when you think about the comparison, houses are a great way to make flips and make money now, but vacant land is the way to build a strong, solid, easy, growing retirement plan.

Now, how about the historical upward value trend of land? Hasn't land always gone up no matter where it is located? I do not care if it is in the middle of the swamp or if it is in the middle of downtown Miami, eventually land will go up. Right?

I actually believe -- and this is terrible to say -- that in the middle of swampland there will be houses someday. It is sad to say, but I believe swampland will have high-rise apartment buildings, businesses, etc. It is really unfortunate. The truth is that our planet is shrinking very fast because of how many people are being born.

Land value will always go up, but you want it to go up in a relatively short time, not 30 to 40 years from now. Do not buy $500 lots on gravel roads with no utilities, no growth and no amenities. Yes, you can make money on it. Obviously this $500 lot can go to $1,000. That is 100% return. But you have got to focus on a specific price range and specific amenities to be able to get results in a reasonable amount of time.

THE PROPER WAY TO BUY LAND

Buy Small, Not Large

I learned the next tip the hard way. It took me years to figure it out. Here is something that I do not want you to do: Do not buy large parcels unless you are a developer. Why not?

Buying large parcels takes time and work and becomes a job. It is not a passive thing. It is something you have to get involved in on a daily basis. You may need to have the land re-zoned. You may have to find a developer that will build houses for you. You will tie up your money to put in roads, sewers, and so on. If you buy a large parcel of land to turn around and sell, you will discover that it is more difficult to sell 500 acres than it is to sell a quarter acre. There are many more people who can afford to buy a quarter acre than can afford 500 acres.

I have several clients who in the past have bought large parcels that have gone up in value, but they have a hard time selling them because they can't find anyone to come up with $300,000 to buy their property.

If they had purchased quarter acre lots, they would have the ability to sell them much more easily because more people can afford a $10,000 lot than can afford a $300,000 large parcel of land. So buying large parcels, unless you are a developer, does not make sense.

Do not buy 10 acres. Do not buy 5 acres. Do not buy 2 acres. Is it possible to make money on those? Sure you can, but is that the best way? Usually not.

Do not buy lots on a golf course or lake. Why not buy lots on the golf course and lake? I have many years of experience with this issue.

For one reason, they are the most expensive. When you resell them, you will have trouble finding people who can afford the property.

Let's say you buy a lot on the golf course that you like; you love the view; it is beautiful; you would live there. You could buy a lot on a golf course for $100,000 and five years later try to sell it at double that price. It is generally much more difficult to sell a lot for $200,000 than for $20,000. So you would be better off using your $100,000 to buy 10 lots at $10,000 each and then selling those lots at $20,000 each. You get the same return, but you have something that every person can afford to buy. Most people can afford a $100 a month payment!

Your customer is going to like property that they can afford, and they are going to like property that already has the amenities, paved roads and other homes in the neighborhood -- right now, today.

I am sharing these key points with you because I do not want you to make the same mistakes I did. Do not buy lots on a golf course. Do not buy lots on a lake.

Golf course lots and lake lots do go up in value, but they are very difficult to sell. If you can sell them, it is much harder for your buyer to continue making monthly payments on a larger note. This is a risk you do not want if you are holding the note.

The Magic Number

Do not buy expensive lots above $20,000. Why is $20,000 so important? I have done this for twenty-four years, long enough to know that any lot $20,000 or less typically does not drop in value. If I buy a lot for $15,000 or $18,000, I probably do not have to worry about the value of it falling to $9,000. If I buy a lot for $35,000 or $45,000, my downside risk goes up. At the same time, my potential for gain goes down.

When the cost for a land parcel reaches $60,000, $70,000, or $80,000 in, let's say, Tennessee -- that is too late to buy. You missed the boat when prices were $5,000, $10,000 or $15,000. You should have bought when prices were at those levels. I have received ads in the mail about land in Tennessee for seven years. Seven years ago when lots were $5,000, I was unsure and did not move on the investment. But had I bought then at $5,000 and sold today at $45,000 to $75,000, I would be a hero. I would have over a <u>500</u> percent return. But I was afraid. "Why would I buy a $5,000 lot in Tennessee," I asked. Looking back, I will never make that mistake again.

If I were to buy lots in Tennessee for $70,000 a lot and wanted to sell at 100 percent return, I would have to sell the lots at $140,000. How many people in America can afford $140,000, especially when lenders typically do not lend on land at all? If they do, they only lend 40 or 50 percent loan to value, if you are lucky! This is why you should stay away from expensive lots.

Remember, anything under $20,000 seems to hold its value. When I started buying lots for $35,000 and $40,000, I started experiencing the volatility of higher-priced land and started having problems with the downside.

I figured out another secret: Do not buy lots that do not have an established infrastructure. New builder development? Areas that do not have an established infrastructure? No way. None of those lots are something that I would buy, even if they are low in price because of the bad economy. It is possible to make money in these areas, but you will have a better chance of re-selling the lot if the infrastructure and amenities are already in place.

Selling a piece of land is all chance, isn't it? We are taking a risk. We are placing a bet. We are saying, "I bet that this quarter acre lot I bought for $10,000 will sell at $20,000 easier than this lot for $100,000 will sell for $200,000." So, betting on a $10,000 lot that has amenities and an infrastructure will probably give you a better chance to make money later on.

What can an average person afford to buy from you when you are ready to sell? Can your buyer afford to make the payments? Remember, if you become the bank and you sell your land and collect the payments of $100 a month from your buyer that is 11 or 12 or 13 percent interest. That is terrific. That can be done on small priced lots. It is very difficult to collect payments on a $300,000 lot because it is hard to collect $3,000 a month from most people. People do not have $3,000 a month to give you on a lot that does not produce income. But on a small priced lot, an average person can buy the lot from you and make payments as low as $98 a month. Nearly everyone can afford that payment. So that is why you stick with lower-priced lots. That is the real end result.

When you become a landlord of land, and you sell off your lots and create an income, then what happens? You do not have to worry about too many defaults because you will have low payments from your buyer. But if the payments are $3,000 a month for a large parcel, the chances of your buyer defaulting are much greater.

Quarter Acres Are the Key

Here is the most important thing to remember. Invest only in quarter acre lots; not an acre, not two acres, but quarter acre as mentioned. Why is it important to invest in quarter acre lots only? They are much easier to sell. A quarter acre lot fits one home nicely. A regular standard home fits on a quarter acre. If it is smaller than a quarter acre, for example, half that size, that is too small. I would not buy those, if I were you. They have to be about a quarter acre because you can fit a nice sized home on the lot that any average person can afford. That is one of my secrets. Make sure they are quarter acres lots and not 5 or 10 acres.

Quarter acre is the key. It does not matter if it is pie-shaped or square. It makes no difference. It does not matter if there are 50 trees or 80 trees or no trees. It does not matter if the lot is sloped up or sloped down, sloped to the left, sloped right. It makes no difference as long as it is a buildable lot. You are buying the subdivision, the area and the amenities. Does the subdivision have value? Will the subdivision go up in value? Does it have amenities? That is what is important.

So quarter acre lots are the secret. That is it; no larger. Stick with this system, and it works every single time.

Invest in the Interior Lots Only

I have purchased many lots on golf courses and lakes -- and for good prices, too. Even though the prices were good, I found out it was a mistake. I can get great prices on lake and golf course lots. But I will not touch them with a 10-foot pole. There is no reason that I, nor you, need to take a risk for $60,000 on a golf course lot or a lake lot when it could drop to $40,000 or $50,000 quite easily.

You should only invest in interior lots, not lake and golf course lots. You are not buying this lot for yourself or for the view. Let's suppose you said to me, "Mike, I want to find a lot because I'd like to have a second home some day in the woods or the mountains." All right. I understand that. But you do not buy your dream lot until you are ready to build on it. In other words, do not buy a lot now because five years later, you may move to another state to have a second home. Buying a lot for yourself years before you are ready to live there is not the best investment. You may change your mind five years from now. If you want to resell that lot and no one else wants it because it is too expensive, then you have wasted time and money.

Invest in lots for investment purposes now and when you decide to finally move, look for the lot of your dreams. Pick a lot on the water or on the golf course, pay full price and move on. But for investment purposes, do not waste time trying to figure out if the lot looks good or if the view is fabulous. The things you need to know before buying investment property are: If the area is growing, if the lots are the right size (remember quarter acre lot size), if there are houses in the area, and if there are amenities in the development.

The Importance of Amenities

I cannot stress to you the importance of amenities. I am telling you that amenities are the key to making this system work. If there are no golf courses, lakes, swimming pools or tennis courts in that subdivision, it is not going to be worth the investment. You need numerous amenities. I do not mean one golf course or one pool. I am talking about enough to make sure that any person who is considering buying your lot can have fun today. Your buyers want to be able to move in now, knowing that the amenities were established years earlier.

I am not talking about a brand new subdivision or developer's site. I never go into a new builder's development, because that is where you get  hung out to dry. Here's why: if it does not work out and the builder does not finish the project, you are stuck with a useless lot. You will lose money. Do not purchase in new builder subdivisions; they are the wrong way to go. I do not care if they are offering financing. I do not care if they give you a 100 percent loan. I do not care if they guarantee you two years worth of rental income. I do not care.

Stay with the quarter acre buildable lots in resort communities that have been around for years and are being advertised on national television.  These infomercials can get your subdivision national exposure, which will increase your lot value. In time, properties that are being marketed on television or areas that have high growth will give you the best results. Why? They are marketing on television to everyone all over the country. So they are telling everyone to come and buy in a subdivision where you own your lots. That will make your value go up eventually and should give you the best results. TV ads will motivate people to investigate subdivisions where you own lots.

Explosive Development

Only invest in resort communities with an established infrastructure and explosive development. Why do you need explosive development? What does that do for the chances of your lot going up in value? Explosive development is retail and commercial development. It is Walmarts, retail stores, schools, etc.

I only look for resort communities where this type of growth is happening. Does that give us a better chance to have more people move there? Does that give us a better chance to have your lot go up in value? Yes!

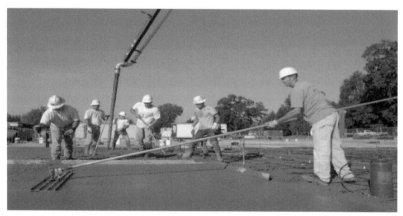

What if you bought a lot and it was the first lot in the subdivision? You would pay a reasonable price, wouldn't you? Now, what if houses were built all around your lot and, at the end of 5 years, your lot was the last vacant lot in the subdivision? What would happen to your lot price? It would skyrocket. But the fact is you took the risk of being the first one to buy a lot. I do not mean the first one at $500 when it is gravel. I am talking about the first lot after the infrastructure is finished and the amenities are there. That is when you want to be first. Not first at $500 in the middle of tumbleweeds. We do not invest in tumbleweeds.

Invest Where the Demand Increases

Invest in areas that have not seen false appreciation. For example, let's talk about Florida and Tennessee. You might know about Florida. We could have bought Florida lots at $5,000. We could have bought them at $10,000. We could have bought them at $15,000, and we could have made money. But if we would have bought them at $60,000, $70,000, $80,000 or $90,000, then we would have lost money. That would have been foolish, because we waited until everyone said, "Buy lots in Florida," before we made the decision. That is usually too late. When you hear everyone bought lots in Florida that means you are the last to the party. The party starts at $5,000, not at $70,000. The party is over at $70,000. You need to arrive at $5,000. That is the beginning of the run.

This is important -- if the lot that you bought for $5,000 did not go up in value for five years, and then finally it doubles after five years, approximately what have you made per year? You have made approximately twenty percent. Let's use the worst case scenario. Let's suppose your lot took 10 years to double. You made approximately 10 percent a year for 10 years, which is a 100 percent return.

If I bought a lot in a subdivision where the infrastructure was completed, homes were already built, amenities were available, and even with explosive growth, it still took 10 years to double my money, I do not care. I just made 10 percent profit per year, which still beats a mutual fund and still has low downside risk. I do not want the risk of a downside. I do not mind 10 percent return on investment, if that is all I get. I will take it. I am okay with that.

I would prefer to have my lots double in three or four years. What return would you be making then? Thirty percent? That is very possible. Most of the lots double in three to five years in a good market. I know that because I have paid more every year for the last six years. Every single year I pay 10 to 20 percent more for the same size lot in the same subdivision.

What is 20 percent more on a $5,000 lot? It is $1,000. If I bought a lot last year for $5,000, this year I would be paying $6,000. Next year I will be paying about $7,200, and the year after $8,600 and so on. You get the idea? In other words, my cost has gone up every year by 20 percent, which means the lots I bought earlier have gone up 20% each year. That gives me the comfort level I need to keep buying, knowing that I can still make money.

Soon the cheaper lots are purchased, and the bottom is bought out over time because it is being advertised on TV. Soon the demand continues and prices rise. It is automatic. It is like that in any subdivision you invest in America. The demand increases over time in areas where there are amenities and growth. It does not happen overnight, because there are plenty of lots in those subdivisions, but it does happen progressively throughout the years.

What if a lot did not go up in value in one year but went up the next year? Isn't that just as good? It does not have to go up consistently every year. You can't be impatient with land. Your chances of gain are still better than with most mutual funds and stocks.

BUYING LAND THE EASY WAY

We Do the Research

Through extensive research, we locate the fastest-growing resort communities and choose only the best for investment. We find out exactly what is going on in these subdivisions before we invest.

Our research department calls planning and zoning departments to find out how many permits were pulled this month compared with how many permits were pulled last month and the year before. We want to know if the roads will be widened and what businesses such as Walmart, grocery stores, drugstores, etc. will be a part of the community. That is how lots increase in value. Our research department does the legwork, so you do not have to.

Our research department's job is to inspect the property for you. For example, we send an associate out to look at the lot to make sure it is buildable. Then we make sure it has clear title and that it is on a paved road with utilities within the subdivision. That means you do not have to fly there and go driving around for days in a subdivision. It is unnecessary. It can be done for you. If it passes our inspection, it is good enough for your portfolio. If there is a problem -- meaning it has a title problem or it is too small -- then we pass on it.

We are always making offers on lots on a recurring basis. They are inspected, and then we purchase them. Remember, as I mentioned previously, all of the lots are about a quarter acre and all look the same. They are all wooded lots. There is nothing tricky about it. There are no dangers, no worries, no risk. We only buy buildable lots.

Let's say you want to buy a property in another state. Is it necessary to drive hours to see a property when it is just a piece of land with trees on it? No. You can easily see pictures of it from Google Earth.

The communities we invest in include established infrastructures only -- lakes, golf, resort amenities and more. We do not go into a subdivision that has one pool, one golf course and one clubhouse. That is not a resort community. There are plenty of those. I want to go into subdivisions that have three, four or five golf courses, three, four or five lakes, and marinas. I want boat ramps and boat rentals. I want a family to be able to buy a lot from you five years from now for $20,000 (that you paid $5,000 for), and be able to have fun immediately. They can go boating, play golf or have the kids swim in the swimming pools today and not have to wait for the builder to finish it all out. That is an easy sell.

If I am going to place a bet, I would rather bet on a subdivision that has amenities and growth. By growth, I mean people moving in and houses being built. I do not want to buy in a subdivision that is sitting idle and empty. I want roads to be paved and utilities nearby. I want to be sure that I am going to make money in my lifetime. If I want to make it happen during that time, I have got to invest now. I cannot wait 30 or 40 more years for the land to increase in value. I have got to have all my investments in line. That is the kind of opportunity I am looking for.

In Lago Vista, Texas, there is a huge lake called Lake Travis. Austin is just next door. How much are lots in downtown Austin? Around $100,000. How much are lots out in the middle of the cornfield where there are tumbleweeds and no paved roads? About

$500. Do I buy lots in the cornfield? No. Do I buy lots in Austin? No. I buy them right in the path of growth, in Lago Vista, for under $20,000. There are fifteen miles of shoreline on Lake Travis. There are marinas already in place.

So this is already a well established community. If people want to fish, there are fishing tournaments all year round. People can move here and have fun today. There are three golf courses. There is also a winery and wildlife refuges and so on. People can live here, drive to Austin in 20 minutes and, best of all, not have to spend $100,000 on a lot. That is another one of my secrets.

Think Like an Investor, Not an Owner

Think like an investor, not an owner. You are an investor, and you are going to have to figure out who would want to buy your lots down the road. What will they be looking for? Good economy, huge growth, low taxes, low insurance, low cost of living, low cost to acquire a lot from you without a loan. For example, a lender does not need to give your buyer a loan for your lot, because your buyer can probably afford to put a $10,000 deposit on your $20,000 lot, and you can finance the rest. They can easily put it on a credit card or borrow from family members. They do not have to go through the loan process for a low-priced lot. On the other hand, if you sold an expensive lot for $200,000, the loan may get denied by the bank three or four times, which ties up your money forever.

Less expensive lots are a better investment because lower priced lots will double in value faster than more expensive lots. For example, a $5,000 lot will increase to $10,000 faster than a $100,000 lot will increase to $200,000. I did not learn this secret until I did it wrong about 50 times. When I figured out the secret, I had already wasted a tremendous amount of money by buying expensive lots. From my experience, the only way to make money in real estate is acknowledging this principle: Lower priced lots will double faster than high priced lots. That is another one of my secrets. There are more buyers who can buy a lot at $10,000 from you that you paid $5,000 for, than can afford to buy a lot at $200,000 that you paid $100,000 for.

Different Ways to Buy a Property

You have options on how to buy a property: There are self-directed IRAs, 1031 exchanges and conventional bank loans. Let's talk about IRAs first. You can buy land in many different ways. Let's say you have $2,000 in your IRA. Can you still buy a piece of land for $15,000? Yes. Let me explain. You can use $2,000 from your IRA and partner with yourself outside of your IRA for the difference. You can use your IRA with $2,000, and partner with your spouse or your spouse's IRA or someone else's IRA or your LLC. You can use your IRA and partner with your corporation, or partner with your partner's corporation, or partner with your spouse's corporation.

If you want to buy five lots and you only have enough money for one, can you still buy lots using means other than your IRA? Yes, you can. You can combine your IRA with any other system you want. You can use three IRAs to buy a lot. You can have two IRAs and one LLC and combine funds to buy a lot. So what if a lot is $15,000, and you only have $2,000 in your IRA? Can you still buy it? Absolutely. Your IRA should be your main focus to get financing.

Many people put CDs and bonds in an IRA. CDs and bonds in an IRA are a joke because you are not making money on the CDs and bonds anyway, so why would you want to have a tax shelter for them? Why put investments that do not make much interest in an IRA? CDs and bonds go outside the IRA and real estate goes inside the IRA. Everyone has it backwards. Your CDs, bonds, and mutual funds (and anything else that does not make money) should go outside your IRA. Your real estate, whether it is homes, shopping centers, or land should go in your IRA.

You will achieve massive wealth ten times faster by investing in your IRA than by investing outside your IRA because you are using the government's money year after year to buy more properties. By buying more properties you are absolutely exponentially growing your IRA rather than outside the IRA, where it is taxed and taxed. If you are taxed outside the IRA, you can't use that money for more land and properties because it is getting taken by the IRS. Use the IRA to protect your profits.

If I were to ask most people what return they are getting in their IRA, most people would tell me, "I don't know," or "It is in mutual funds," or "I have no idea. I don't even look at it." They are saying that because it is their IRA, it is for retirement and doesn't concern them now. If it is for retirement, you better look at it today. You are probably not getting the best benefit from your IRA. If you use your IRA as your tool to leverage yourself now in a tax-free vehicle, you will experience a retirement that is financially stress-free.

What if you said to me, "I understand IRAs, but I do not want to have all this money in an IRA when I can't get to it until I am 59-1/2."

Well, that is not true; you can take money out of your IRA early. You just have to pay a penalty. I have made millions in IRAs, and I have taken money out of them early. Why? If I can increase my IRA fund from $10,000 to $1 million by being a landlord of land, then if I take it out and pay taxes and a $100,000 penalty, I still end up ahead. Am I better off than somebody else? Sure. I do not care about the penalty. I will pay the penalty if I am only 50 years old. Now, to be sure, I am going to keep my money in the IRA until I need it. But, if I need to take money out of the IRA for any reason at all, I will take some out and pay the penalty. Whatever reason you have to take it out early, it won't hurt that much to take it out and pay the penalty and taxes. If you have made millions in your IRA because you focused on building wealth now and did not wait until later when you are 62 to try to figure out what to do, you will have plenty of money to pay a small penalty.

You are responsible for your destiny. No one else is. You are responsible for getting to the finish line and being self-sufficient, being able to do what you want to do, when you want to do it. You are reading this book because you want to secure your future. You are not reading this because you need the biggest house or the most toys; that is not what it is about. You want to secure your future, make sure your family is secure regardless of your health problems or anything that might go wrong.

No one wants to start over. Pay attention to your IRA today. Think about it, figure out how to increase funds in your IRA and contribute every chance you get. Even if you do not have enough money in your IRA, borrow money to buy land, combine money with other IRAs or partner with partners outside the IRA if you have to and make it happen.

1031 Exchange into Vacant Lots

Let's talk about 1031 exchange. You can transition from any property or real estate into land. You can sell a house or a shopping center and purchase lots. You can sell a shopping center for a million dollars and purchase 500 quarter acre single lots, if you want to. That is how you diversify.

Conventional Bank Loans

Getting a conventional bank loan for land is not something that I recommend for people who are the faint of heart. But I can tell you that this is how I built my land portfolio into hundreds of lots. For example, I borrowed money on my home equity line of credit.

Let's suppose you can obtain a $100,000 home equity line-of-credit at 6 percent. If you borrow money at 6 percent and you sell your lots at 12.9 percent, you are basically using the bank's money to create a spread. In other words, if you are borrowing money at 6 percent, your payment on a lot might be $89 a month whereas your income could be $227 from your seller-held note. You have a lot more coming in than actually going out because your equity line is long-term and your new buyer's loan is short-term. He is paying higher payments to you than you are paying to the bank. You are paying a lower rate than the buyer. It is a significant difference from $227 income in your IRA versus $89 going out to your bank.

And if your buyer does not pay you the monthly payments, what happens? You still owe the bank for the loan, and you still have to pay your monthly payments.

If you are selling ten lots to individuals, and you are collecting income from all 10 people, if one of those 10 people does not pay you, the other nine make up the difference. You never have to dip into your pocket to pay that 6 percent loan. You can borrow money on an equity line at 6 or 7 percent for any property that you own and loan it out by buying land and selling it the next day. What if you bought a lot for $5,000 with the bank's money, and sold it for $5,000 the next day at 12 percent interest? If you want to wait, wait. But if you want to buy a lot today and sell it tomorrow at 12 percent and collect the interest, you can do that.

That is how you can acquire 100 lots in the next 10 years. But that is not something you do until you feel totally comfortable. Do not borrow money for land until you feel comfortable, because it is not for the faint hearted. If you have not mastered the process of selling land, you should not borrow money to buy land! If you do not do it right, you will be making payments on your own. So hold off until you understand the process of borrowing money and reselling the land.

The Simple System

These are the rules that you have to follow. Follow the system because it works every time. How much effort does it take for a parcel of land to increase from $5,000 to $10,000? Do you have to build a house? Do you have to do repairs? Do you have to handle calls from anyone? No. There is nothing to do to get this reward. Nothing but sit and wait. Just close on the lot and hold it long-term. That is another one of my secrets.

Expensive lots stay on the market longer, tying up your initial investment. If someone put a contract on your lot for $200,000 and needed bank financing, you essentially are waiting for them to get approved. Months go by; the prospective buyer is denied a loan. What happens? Now you have got to put it back on the market, show it again for another three, four or five months or even a year, trying to find another buyer and hoping they get approved. Good luck.

But on a low priced lot, if someone says, "I'll buy your lot for $10,000" and you paid $5,000 for it, isn't it easier to get a loan? A bank will give a loan on $10,000 for a lot because the buyer usually has that much in collateral. They probably have stocks, bonds or an IRA. They can use their IRA to buy a lot from you for $10,000.

Return on Investment

Return on investment is also important. Less expensive lots offer a greater chance for a larger percentage return. For example: To get 20 percent return in a year on a $100,000 lot, you have got to sell it and net $120,000. You have got to net $20,000 profit after taxes, Real Estate fees, closing costs, etc. That is your 20 percent gain. To make the same 20 percent return on a $5,000 lot you only need to sell it for $6,000 net after taxes and fees. Don't you think you could sell a lot for $6,000 easier than $120,000? Absolutely. It is much easier to find buyers for a $6,000 lot.

You could buy 20 lots at $5,000 each and sell each of those for $6,000 and net 20 percent profit easier than buying a $100,000 lot and trying to sell it for $120,000, because not only is it too expensive, but you also run the risk that your buyers will get turned down over and over again by the bank.

Eventually, if your lot doubles in five years, what return do you make? One hundred percent, right? So if you make 100 percent return in five years, what is that average per year? Approximately twenty percent a year. That is a great return. What if your lot took 10 years to double? What is the return on interest per year? It is approximately ten percent a year. Compare that to mutual funds. What do you get in mutual funds in a year, if you are lucky? Twelve, 11, 10, 9 percent -- that is if the fund does not go down.

Invest in affordable lots between $5,000 and $20,000. I know we can find lots for $500 or $1,000, but they are usually on gravel roads, have title problems, no utilities or they are not near amenities. I do not buy those lots. We never purchase lots that are too cheap with no upside potential. Stay with lots between $5,000 and $20,000. You are safer on the downside and have a much greater chance to profit on the sale in a reasonable amount of time.

HOW TO SELL LOTS

Let's talk about how you sell lots. You may be saying, "Great. I can easily buy a lot. However, that is not the hard part. How do I sell a lot?" Let's say it is in a different state and you do not have any contacts in that state. I will be glad to give you any contacts that can help you sell your lot when you are ready. There are several different exit strategies. Let's take a look at some of them.

The first strategy is short-term and flip. That means you are in the land business. If you want to actually do this for a business, then you would flip lots. That is not what I recommend. That is not how you make the most money.

The second exit strategy is to wait for the lot to appreciate in value and then sell it. This is where the third strategy comes in.

The third exit strategy is to owner-finance the lot for income, and that makes you a landlord of land. You sell lots to someone else who puts either zero down -- or whatever you agree to -- and your buyer makes payments to you at 10 to 13 percent interest. Isn't that a good return on your money? You do not want to do this until these lots have appreciated, because if a lot can go up 20 percent a year for several years, it may then start to slow down. That is when you finance your lot and collect the income and become a landlord of land. You are getting the profit from the sale of your lot, plus interest on that profit. By charging interest on your lot over time to your buyer, you are making significantly more profit on the lot than if you sold it for cash.

If you were to sell your lot right now and make only 20 percent gain, you are just moving money around. There is no reason to do that. You make the most money by allowing your lot to appreciate over time. Hold onto the lots for three, four or five years and then consider selling them when they reach $30,000, $40,000, or $50,000, and you can collect interest income per month.

If you had 100 lots that you bought over 10 years and were collecting $200 a month from your buyers, how much is that per month? One hundred lots at $200 a month per lot is $20,000 a month with no maintenance, no tenants, no repairs, no phone calls, no headaches, and zero to do. What have you had to do so far? Nothing. That is the idea. You do not want to be an owner financer until the lots have appreciated and you can realize a gain. Once you have realized your gain and the property starts to slow down in appreciation, then sell the lot and lock-in your seller financing strategy. Otherwise, if you sell that lot too soon, using seller-held financing, you have stopped your potential gain.

Who Will Buy Your Lot?

Who is going to be buying your lots 5 or 10 years from now? Obviously, baby boomers and builders. Think about it. A builder may call you five years from now and offer you double for your lot. Does that mean you have to sell it just because the price doubled? If you bought a lot at $5,000, does that mean you have to sell it for $10,000? No. Everyone says, "Oh, I doubled my money." But why not wait until it goes to $20,000 or $25,000, and sell when it starts to slow down in appreciation? What happens if it goes to $45,000? Doesn't it make sense to hold your land as long as you can, unless you need the money for desperate reasons? In other words, hold your land!

Baby boomers are moving from northern states, and they are looking to retire in places with a warmer climate. They do not have to move to Florida. They can move to Texas, Arkansas, Georgia, or the Carolinas. In Florida, they have high cost of insurance, high cost of taxes, and high cost of land. Can you find a piece of land anywhere in Florida for $5,000? No! There could be land for sale on Mars right now for $5,000, but you are not going to want that. You need something that is going to go up in value during your lifetime, right?

People have a choice to move to Florida and worry about hurricanes and the high cost of living, or they can move to other southern states and purchase lots with amenities. They can't buy a lot in Fort Lauderdale for $5,000. It is not possible. Do you have to buy in Florida? No. Because all those people up north -- baby boomers -- are going to be moving to other states. It is seasonal. The southern states still have some warm weather, and it is better than snow every day. People still get beautiful weather and they can enjoy their retirement.

Builders may want to buy lots from you two or three at a time. I constantly have builders calling me and saying, "Mike, I'd like to buy three of your lots." I can obviously make 50 percent on my money because I bought them six years ago, but why would I do that if the lot can go from $20,000 to $45,000 in the next five years? I would be foolish to sell them just because they doubled in value. All I have to do is wait. Let the builders keep buying lots and keep building two or three houses at a time on the roads around my lots, and I will get my results later.

What if you could have invested in lots in Florida 10 years ago? Anywhere in Florida. Even without the resorts, even if you did not have amenities, you still could have made money. But the fact is now it is expensive. It is a dangerous gamble now that prices are much higher. Keep your risk lower by investing in *lower-priced* lots only.

States like Texas and Arkansas are just like Florida was 10 years ago. You can buy lots in Texas near Austin for about $17,000. Those lots are valuable because the value can rise to $40,000 in the next five years. That is easy. The same applies in Arkansas. There are beautiful resorts in Arkansas that are priced just as Florida was 10 years ago. Just think if you would have bought a lot in Cape Coral, Florida for $5,000. You could have made a ton of money on that lot -- $55,000 to $60,000 -- at the top of the market without amenities! Even if you tried to sell it right now in a slow market, you would still be making money. If you bought those lots now, at $50,000, $60,000, or $70,000, you would be foolish. They are priced much too high.

Marketing Your Lot

There are several ways to sell properties that I want to share with you. But first, I want to give you a secret that I use for finding buyers.

Market for buyers before you need them and build a buyers database. If you build a buyers database filled with people who like to buy land, they will become good customers and will come back to you to purchase more land again and again. When you have new lots come into your portfolio and you want to sell them at 11 percent interest, you do so to the same people over and over so that they can build their portfolios. They are making payments to you, they are getting their appreciation, and you are getting the 11 percent interest.

Internet auctions, like eBay. You should always put your land for sale on EBay. You should put land for sale on EBay as long as you still own it and try to get leads. You should always advertise for buyers before you need them. In other words, always market your land for sale to find buyers. Even when you run out of inventory, you still post ads saying, "Lots for sale, zero down, 100 percent financing, no credit check, everyone approved." Will you get calls from that kind of an ad? You better believe it.

Internet classifieds. You should always use Craigslist. It does work. But remember, you have got to maintain your ads. You have got to make sure you keep your ads at the top which takes a little bit of time. For example, you need to refresh your ads every few days by changing a word or two. Even if you do not want to sell your lots now, you should advertise for leads to build your buyers database.

"For sale" sign. This can be placed on a lot by a local person. You do not need to fly to another state to put a "For sale" sign on a property. There is no reason why you should spend any time doing anything but collecting the money. How do you get a "For sale" sign placed on a piece of property that isn't even in your state?

You call the sign company and tell them to print a sign. Should the sign say "Coldwell Banker - For sale - call Mary"? No. That is not a sign. That is not how a sign works. First of all, it should never say "for sale" because if a sign is on a property, what does it mean? It is for sale. So why do you have to write it on there? Do not waste space. It should not say "For sale, call Michael." It should say, **"Zero down, 100 percent financing, no credit check, everyone approved," and a phone number.** You do not need a name. You do not need "For sale." Your sign company will print the sign, and you pay the sign company or the realtor $100 to put it on the property. It takes them five minutes. If you want proof of the work, have them take a picture and email it to you.

Then you pay a realtor to make sure it is on the right property. This is in case the sign company put it on the wrong property in error. These are mistakes that I learned the hard way. I would get calls for a lot I did not own. I wondered, "How did this happen to me?" Time was wasted, time was lost, money was lost. To avoid this, ask a realtor to come and check on it.

When a realtor goes to check on your property, ask them to take a digital photo of your property and e-mail it to you. Now you have a photo that can be used for your advertising. The photo can be used for eBay, Craigslist or newspaper ads, etc.

Think about how to get things done the smart way. Work smarter, not harder. Now you have a photo of the lot that can be used in whatever way you need.

Newspaper classified ads. You should always have ads in the newspaper, even if you do not have any inventory. Always. Why? Because you want to find out who wants to buy vacant land, homes or commercial real estate. Run ads in the *Chicago Tribune, New York Times*, etc. Do not just run ads in the local paper. Why can't you run an ad in a Chicago newspaper looking for investors wanting land in Texas? Why can't you print **"Land for sale in Texas"** or **"Land for sale in Arkansas, zero down, 100 percent financing, no credit check, everyone approved,"** and your phone number in an ad in the *Chicago Tribune* or *New York Times*? Will you get calls from that kind of an ad? How about 80 calls in two weeks? Eighty calls in two weeks from people who potentially would love to own a piece of land, and even though they do not have the money for a full purchase, they could make payments. That is a great response!

This system is how you sell properties in 6 months or less instead of on the MLS like everyone else. Do not use the MLS solely to sell properties. The MLS alone will not do. Do not use just one marketing strategy. Use all of the strategies for the best results.

Personal web pages. If you put up a one-page website that lists properties for sale and have to pay $50 to $100 a month to optimize it on Google, is it worth it? Yes. You must do marketing. You can't expect land to sell by just putting up a "For sale" sign and letting it die on the vine. That is the wrong way. You need multiple ways to find buyers, and you want to find buyers all the time. This advertising goes on constantly. You keep your ads even when you have nothing for sale.

I have accumulated 10,000 people in my database in seven years just for real estate. I ran newspaper ads, collected thousands of business cards from every event I have ever attended, and I ran ads on Craigslist and eBay. That is how you build a database.

Real estate agents. Can you sell your lots at zero down using a realtor? Yes. Why would a realtor sell your vacant lot if there is going to be no money transacted at closing? Why would a realtor sell your lot at zero down, 100 percent financing? Why would a realtor do that if they think they can't get paid? They wouldn't, unless you can pay them. You tell a realtor, "I want you to sell my lot, and if you sell it, your commission will be $500 a lot." If you sell it, there is no commission to the realtor. That is rule number one. Never, ever give an exclusive to a realtor. I am a realtor, and I know better. Never give an exclusive to a realtor for a piece of land. Ever. Another way to pay your realtor is on terms from the monthly income you receive from your buyer's monthly payment.

The realtor might say, "Well, I am going to market it and advertise it." Okay. Great. You offer them double the commission. A typical commission on a vacant lot is about $500. That is usually what a realtor makes on a quarter acre lot. It is not a lot of money, but they sell many of them all the time. They are making good money per week. If you offer a realtor $1,000, are they going to sell your lot first or someone else's? And if you offer a realtor $1,000 for a lot that they can sell to someone who does not have any money -- zero down, 100 percent financing, no credit check -- can't that realtor sell that lot faster than any other lot in the whole subdivision?

I do not care if there are five thousand lots for sale in the subdivision. I do not care because a realtor can sell your lot first because they have the ability to sell it with the best terms, and they are getting paid double the commission. They have the best terms in the world.

You are going to price your lot not at the market price, but just below it. Never price your lot higher because when you price it higher, you cut yourself out of the game. Price your lot just below the market and stick to your price rather than price it higher and play the game. You are better off pricing it lower to get the buyer in the door quickly. Price it low enough to sell.

If it does not sell right away, what do you do? Wait. That is all, just wait. Let it appreciate and eventually it will take care of itself. As people keep moving from the north to the south, your lots will go up in value because homes are built in these subdivisions every day.

The Stress-Free Landlord

Following this system allows you to be a landlord without the headaches. You do not have any tenants; that is obvious. Only vacant land does not require tenants or upkeep of the property. You can do what you enjoy everyday and not have to worry about the land. There are no structures to maintain or insure. You do not need insurance when you own lots in an LLC or in your IRA.

There are lower taxes on vacant land than there are on a home. How much are taxes on a quarter acre per year? About $25.00 or less. The taxes on a home will cost $3,000, $4,000, or $6,000 per year. The tax on vacant land is only around $25.00 because it is raw land that has not been developed. Your taxes are not expensive. Your land is tax deductible; it is something you can write off.

A contract to sell your land is called a contract for deed. You can either use a regular mortgage, or you can use a contract for deed, if it is legal in your state. Contract for deed means you maintain control of the land the entire time. If your buyer defaults, you simply send legal notice of time to cure the default. If the buyer defaults, you resell the lot to a different buyer at the new, higher price.

Seller Financing

Let's suppose you decide to sell off your lots using seller-held notes, and you are collecting $200 a month. One of your buyers stops paying you after two or three years. They paid you $200 every month until suddenly they decide they are in a bind and can't afford to pay you anymore. You are still in control, aren't you? In addition, they paid you all that time and your lot has probably gone up in value. You take the lot back through a simple foreclosure process -- not a difficult one like a home -- and you resell the lot at a higher price, and you have made money all that time.

Is there any risk of a default? Who cares? I do not care what the buyer's credit is. I do not care if they have made payments all their life. When I advertise a lot for sale, it is zero down, 100 percent financing, no credit check, everyone is approved. Does that get buyers? Absolutely.

If you bought a lot at $5,000 using your IRA, and three or four years later you sold it for $8,000, what percent return is that? Sixty percent. Is this feasible? Sure it is. Is it possible to go from $5,000 to $8,000 in five years, three years, or even two years? Sure it is. Absolutely. Compare that return to mutual funds. Can you get that in mutual funds in two to three years? Not likely!

Let's say you sold a lot at 11 percent interest over a five year loan. If someone was going to make payments to you, the payments would be $85 a month. Why would someone pay you 11 percent to have the right to put zero down on your lot with bad credit? Here is why: You are giving them the ability to avoid a credit check and not have the transaction show up on a credit report at all – your seller financing loan never shows up on a credit report. They are paying you $85 a month. An average person can afford this! That is why this system works. It is affordable for everyone.

Here is another example. You buy a lot for $15,000 using your IRA and sell it at $21,900. That is a 45 percent return, *a phenomenal return*. There is actually no downside risk. You could collect $227 a month at 11 percent over a five year loan. In five years they pay you in full. Then, you are done. If they stop paying you $227 a month, what do you do? Resell the property at a higher price. How about selling it at $24,900 or $29,900 or even more? You continue to gain the appreciation all that time while being a landlord of land.

If a buyer defaults, it can actually be a good thing. Doesn't it make sense to offer someone zero down, 100 percent financing, no credit check, everyone approved? Why? Because you have no risk at all. I do not care if they do not pay me down the road. It does not matter to me. That is their mistake. If they want to buy your lot, they should pay you the full amount.

Now, why would someone pay you 11 percent for a lot? If it can go up 20 percent a year and they are paying you 11 percent, isn't it still an advantage to them to pay you for that lot? Sure it is. Everyone wants to own a piece of land; that is the American dream. It is still better than not owning a lot at all. If the lot can go up 20 percent a year, and they are paying you 11 percent interest, it is still worth it. Their lot is paid for in five years and, because it is going up 20 percent a year, it is their profit. It is worthwhile for anybody in America to buy land from you. They can be making 5 per cent each year, even if they pay 15% interest on their loan!

Look what would happen if you bought three lots at $15,000 and sold them for $21,900 using owner financing. You would not only make a profit on the sale, you would also make money on the monthly interest. You are double dipping. You are going to collect your gain of 45 percent, and then owner finance these three lots and collect $684 a month. This $684 a month keeps adding up. What do you do with that money? You buy more lots. Keep adding more real estate to your IRA. The $684 per month is 100 per cent re-usable and gives you huge momentum, more buying power, and no taxes!

If this is going into your Roth IRA, then there are no taxes on the income. How about this: If you bought 10 lots over the next three or four years and you had $2,200 a month coming in from your owner financing, how many more lots could you buy with $2,200 a month?

If they were $5,000 lots, you could buy one every other month. How many can you buy in a year? Nearly six per year. That means your portfolio increases from 10 to 16, from 16 to 22, and from 22 to 28 because you are using the income from all the lots tax-free in your IRA. You are using the income from the 10 lots. Do you follow me? It is a system that continually perpetuates itself in your Roth IRA tax free.

How about this? When you own 100 lots (10 years from now or five years from now), you will be collecting $22,000 a month. Can you live off that, tax free, headache free with no aggravation, stress, tenants or downside risk? I will take that all day long. That is easy, isn't it?

Let's suppose that a few people stop making the payments. You can take the lots back and sell them at a higher price as mentioned previously. If that happens four years later or five years later and that lot has doubled in value, what are you going to make? Now it is a much higher price.

The cash flow you receive from financing vacant lots is only one way to build your IRA rapidly. It does not include the annual contributions from your job or other portfolio assets. You see what I mean? This is just building your IRA from the land itself. This becomes an absolute money tree. If you could have passive income from raw land, isn't that easier than other investments? That is why this works.

Collecting Money

Let me explain to you how easy this process is. Let's suppose I had $22,700 a month coming in. Does that mean I have to collect 100 checks every month? No, this can all be done by using an attorney, CPA, or IRA custodian. At the first of the month all the checks are due. If, in fact, some checks are late, your attorney (or custodian) notices that they are late and takes care of it. You do not have to worry about it. You can be on vacation in Costa Rica or wherever you would like to be. You do not have to be tied to a mailbox to do business. If your buyers do not pay, your attorney or custodian will send a letter of default.

Your attorney or custodian collects the money and deposits it into his escrow account. When the funds clear the bank, he transfers it into your account so that it is in your bank on whatever date you have chosen. If a buyer is late with a payment, the attorney or custodian sends the buyer a letter regarding the past due amount. You do not have to worry about it. You never have to take any phone calls or see the money or deal with anything. You can travel throughout the world and do what you enjoy and not have to be bothered with renters calling. It is on auto-pilot. You do not have to be there to make this happen.

TAX ADVANTAGES OF IRA INVESTING

IRAs offer substantial tax advantages that have made many people wealthy. There are no capital gains tax paid when property is sold by the Roth IRA. Profits from the sale and monthly income are deposited back into the IRA. Not just the profit, not just the income, but <u>both</u> go in your IRA tax free. You are not paying taxes on that $227 a month times 10 lots. Use the tax-free money to do it over and over and become a landlord of land. That is the way real wealth is built. It allows you to enjoy compounded interest to reinvest into other vacant home sites.

All this money coming in tax-free goes into buying more land. Investing in lots offers true diversification in assets instead of stocks, bonds and mutual funds. When you buy vacant lots and buy in more than one area, you are building a mutual fund of land.

Build yourself a portfolio of many low-priced lots. Not a $1 million parcel, but many parcels spread throughout resort communities. Purchasing many parcels throughout several resorts gives you downside protection and diversification at the same time. Spread out your money into different subdivisions, spread out your money into different parcels so that you have the ability to protect your downside and increase your upside.

Be a Landlord of Land

This section explained how you can be a landlord of land -- selling land and collecting ten to twelve percent income, and collecting it on one lot, 50 lots or 1,000 lots. That is how you become so wealthy, with no headaches. It is done every day.

Turnkey Investment Secret Strategy #2

BANK OWNED HOUSES

Turnkey Out of the Box Investment Secret Number Two is about bank-owned houses and duplexes. I'm about to show you a turnkey investment strategy that will teach you how to invest in foreclosed, bank-owned properties directly from banks so that you can free up your time, do a lot more deals and increase your wealth. Banks are, of course, a terrific and plentiful source of properties, many of which you can get at under-market value. Banks are not in the business of owning real estate. They are in the business of managing money. So when properties are foreclosed and end up on the bank's books, they need to clear that deadweight off their accounts.

Dealing with Banks

Yes, banks are going to try to get the most money they can for properties; they are trying to recoup their money on a bad loan. However, there comes a time in a bank's accounting cycle where it needs to get properties off its books no matter what the price. Does this happen only at the end of the year? No. Different forces are constantly at work within the banking structure. Sometimes those forces are changes in banking regulations: Penalties for bad loans are instituted in the form of lowered bank rankings and increased reserve requirements and put pressure on the bank to move the REOs off their books. Code violations or just the responsibility of running properties take their toll.

Banks are a plentiful source of properties but you need to have a relationship with the bank as well as the person inside the bank who is in charge of the properties and, of course, a track record as someone who can close deals.

One of the first obstacles investors run into when trying to buy properties directly from a bank is finding the right person to speak with. If the bank doesn't know you, they will try to pass you on to their real estate agent or some banks will even say they don't have any REOs currently. They don't want to deal with individuals who can't get the deal done. If you do get to the proper person at the bank, you are going to have to negotiate the deal, usually bringing cash to the table. Once you have the property you will have to supervise all the repairs, or worse, do them yourself. If the property is not in an area close to you geographically, you will have to hire crews who you don't know and can't completely trust. Once the property is fixed up, you can list it with a real estate agent or try to rent or sell it yourself. Now you are meeting people at the property, dealing with qualifying buyers or renters, and having all the fun that goes with that.

The Opportunity

Instead of having to do it yourself and struggle with trying to find, negotiate, fix and sell the property on top of figuring the entire process of dealing with banks (and it is a process!) let me show you our system which has a proven track record. We have consistently negotiated and bought nice homes in nice neighborhoods from banks, fixed them and flipped them. I'm sure once you have looked over this program, you will see the benefit of using a turnkey system and will gain a comfort level with this program.

This is a full service, turnkey program. The properties are at about 80 percent of the original cost. At one time, these houses were selling for $200,000 to $250,000. Now, with the decline in the market, we can pick up these houses for next to nothing. Over the past two years, South Florida has undergone a huge real estate market correction. It's a 90-percent correction, one of the biggest in history, and it seems like now is the time to take advantage of this. We are seeing homes that had sold for $300,000 now on the foreclosure market for as low as $65,000 to $100,000 and these are beautiful, beautiful homes.

These low prices combined with low vacancy rental rates give us a perfect niche opportunity. There are so many people who have been displaced who don't have any place to live. Many people are leaving their house where they had been paying on a mortgage, and they're moving next door or down the block, paying $600, $700, $800 a month in rent as opposed to $1,200 or more to a bank. It's a huge opportunity to rent houses almost immediately, within a week or two.

Our goal is to provide investors with a turnkey operation where a team of experts does everything for you including negotiating with the bank and buying the houses direct. The team fixes the house for the investor. Typical repairs are around $5,000 or so, which is mostly for cosmetics. I'll go over that later in this chapter. The team also handles the sales to the end user for the investor. The revenues are shared between the investor and the team.

This is a true partnership program. This program allows you to put money into a partnership, while having someone else do all the work and leverage their established connections with the bank. Our partners know to target the exact houses for our program: Low priced, in basically good condition and inexpensive to fix. They then sell the properties either to a local person or maybe one of our investors from out of the area. We've been giving seminars in different states and different countries to investment groups to find out who is interested in buying. Our buyers' list is continually growing and properties are selling, on average, within about 90 days.

Where the Deals Are

The target area is Lee County, Florida. Lee County is the number one real estate market in the current economic boom/burst. It was one of the hottest areas growing the quickest, the fastest, and then all of a sudden, it got hit the hardest. Now, it's the number one foreclosure market. It went from being the best area to the worst area in just one market cycle. Yet, it's ranked as the number two county in the country for population growth by U.S. census and Forbes Magazine ranked the area as the top county for new businesses.

Lee County is over 1,200 square miles in size. Our main focus is Fort Myers, Cape Coral and Lehigh Acres. Those are the areas that have been hardest hit, that we can take the best advantage of.

Take a look at the map on the next page. You can see that Lehigh Acres is just east of I-75. It's just a little bit further away from the Gulf of Mexico, and then Cape Coral is just a little bit west of I-75, which is a little bit closer to the water and the prices are reflected as such. The Cape Coral area is a little bit more expensive, because most of the properties are either on the water, on canals, or right across the street from water or there is water somewhere nearby. It's also less than 20 minutes from downtown historical Fort Myers, which is going through a $60 million dollar renovation and revitalization plan. It is fifteen minutes from Sanibel Island, all white sand, beautiful beaches, great restaurants. Captiva Island, which is right next to Sanibel, has the same flavor; these are beautiful resort areas. The area is less than 15 minutes from Southwest Florida International Airport so people can fly in and out easily.

The area has all the stores that people want: Wal-Mart, Target, Home Depot. It has shopping centers, restaurant chains, major franchises. There's plenty of shopping, plenty of grocery stores, plenty of places to go eat, plenty of things to do.

Best of all, there's a surplus of foreclosure properties in this area. Just a few years ago, there were tons of houses being built one after another. Now, they're just stacked up by the thousands. There are plenty of properties to choose from, especially when you get them from the bank at those low prices. Preconstruction is at an all-time low. Local economists state that the market is at a bottom pricing. They're thinking that these are the best prices we're going to find, and most likely, eventually, they'll start creeping up again, and we'll end up paying more.

About the Properties and the Market

The rental market is one of the best I've seen. Think about how good it would feel to rent a house in just two weeks or less. That's the way I like to do it. I want the rental income coming in as fast as possible so it does not delay the return on my investment. Again, we are getting these foreclosed homes directly from the banks. They're 2004 or newer. They definitely have some cosmetics to do, such as pressure washing, appliances, sometimes carpeting and paint, maybe landscaping and weed and feed. All of these things are easy, quick and inexpensive to take care of. The places really shine up quite nicely. They look good. They meet all the criteria for the new, current hurricane codes because they were built so recently. Low insurance rates are a definite help. That's an incentive for your buyers.

We do mid-level cosmetic rehabs, no structural rehabs. There's no worrying about any kind of concrete block or steel or any kind of structural grooving. Nothing like that has to be done. We also have third-party inspectors inspect the houses. We want an outside service to come in and put a stamp of approval on the house so that you're not just going by our word. We want to make sure that you see that we not only respect and value other people's opinions but we have the business sense to consult experts to make sure the house is up to snuff.

Only ten percent of these available homes meet our criteria. The properties we choose have to be in great condition and perfect shape. We only take the cream of the crop, and it takes some time to go through those. We have to go through maybe five or ten at a time to see exactly what they look like inside. All properties are always fully inspected by an experienced rehab team prior to being purchased from the banks. That's part of our normal purchasing criteria.

The rehab and inspection team goes through the property with a fine-tooth comb, looking at the wiring, making sure there's no Chinese drywall, checking all the construction, making sure there are no leaks, checking to make sure that the tile, the tubs, everything's in place correctly. Everything has to be done right. That's how you get a house sold quickly. Only the best properties are chosen. If we look at a house, and it's in too bad of shape or has too much damage, or it costs too much to repair, we just pass. No problem. There are plenty of other good, solid houses in the queue.

Our typical rehab includes interior paint, interior cleaning, carpet replacement or maybe just refurbishment, minor landscaping, appliance replacement, and, most of the time, an AC unit. Because our rehab teams are experienced and have systems in place, we are able to minimize the investor's rehab costs while bringing the home back to brand-new condition. It seems to me that because our crews know what they are doing, they can get the home rehabbed more quickly, we can get the house put on the market quicker and get it sold faster. That's how we're hitting those numbers up in 90 days. With a good rehab team, it only takes a week or two to get a property repaired. It doesn't take three or four months like some of the houses you've seen.

This is what I call an easy turnkey investment strategy. The experts know what rehab work will provide the most profitable returns. Instead of over-building and adding on things that would never make the house go up in value, they take care of the basics that get the house to look crisp, clean and better than most of the properties on the market.

On the next page is a typical example of what some of these houses look like. As you can see, these houses are going to need pressure washing, a little landscaping and some cleaning. It'll end up looking very nice, but we are starting with good-looking houses. Finding excellent houses at these low prices is not going to last that long. Eventually, these prices will go away.

The interiors typically have newer kitchens, bathroom vanities, everything is really well done. There are high cathedral ceilings in some. Some have a big whirlpool Jacuzzi, two car garages, nice amenities like that in the single-family homes.

What would it cost to build a home like this today?

Let's say a builder was going to go ahead and build this particular house right now. You've got the cost of the land, $14,000; impact fees, escalation and fill, about $9,000; closing costs on the loan, $6,000; real estate commission to the realtor, $10,800; construction costs, $111,000. You're at $150,000 just to rebuild the same exact house.

To me, that keeps builders out of the building game for quite some time. The cost to build is about double what we are paying. That's good news. That means that we will be able to buy and sell in that area for quite some time without ever having to worry about competition from a brand new home. This is a good time. Here are some examples of what a house would cost and what the typical rehab cost would be. Let's take a look at this.

Let's use $58,000 in this case as our purchase price from the bank, because that's been about normal. Think about it, $58,000 for a nearly new house? That's phenomenal. $58,000 for a beautiful 1,500-square-foot house, three bedrooms, two bathrooms, with a garage. Typical rehab costs run between $4,000 to $6,000, let's say $5,000 on average. Total acquisition cost is $63,000. The property should sell for about $95,000, according to our most recent comps and the most recent properties that we have sold. That means that we're selling them at $55 to $60 per square foot. That's a pretty good profit. The selling commissions and closing costs run about $5,300 on average. The gross profit is $26,700.

The partnership works in this way: Sixty percent goes to the group on the west coast of Florida that does all the work. They find the properties and get them fixed up and sold. Forty percent goes to the investor. That means that 60 percent of the $26,000 would be around $16,000. The other 40 percent or $10,680 would go to the investor. The cash on cash return to an investor is 15 percent every four months. That's on average. What if the investment only turned once every six months? Well, that's two times a year. That's a pretty good return. Thirty percent is difficult to get, especially when you're looking at CDs, bonds, mutual funds or stocks. Those investments are not likely to get that kind of return. This is probably one of the better ways to be more aggressive and get some results. And your risk is limited because you bought the house so cheaply.

Exit Strategies

Now, there are a couple of exit strategies here. **Exit Strategy Number One** is to prepare the house and sell it to a local investor or to a foreign investor looking to invest in Florida. Now, why would a foreign investor invest in Florida? As I mentioned earlier, we do a lot of seminars in other countries. Let's take Germany, for example. In Germany, it would cost $350,000 to buy a house like the one that they could buy in Florida. When they finally realize that it's true, yes, they can buy a house here for that price, they buy one for themselves as a vacation home, and sometimes, they have us rent it out for them. Sometimes, they use the property themselves. It just depends on what they want to do. We have been actively cultivating foreign buyers because as great as the deals are for U.S. buyers, they are phenomenal to foreign nationals!

There is a demand for these properties, especially since they are so close to the Gulf of Mexico. Living twenty minutes from the beach in Lehigh Acres is not bad at all. It's even better in Cape Coral -- only ten minutes from the beach. The location is ideal, absolutely ideal. As I said, the average time on the market for a sale is right around 90 days, sometimes up to 120 days. The average profit per house is $25,000 or $26,000. There have been over 200 homes bought and sold over the last two years. Definitely, there's a track record there. And, full disclosure: Yes. You make money on some, and some, you do not. But if you have 10 houses, and you can make money on seven or eight or nine out of 10, that's gravy. That's all gravy. And that's how it works.

Exit Strategy Number Two is to rehab and rent the property out to a good local family who has lost their home due to the downturned market and let them live in a house that is almost comparable to the one they've just lost. They like that. They feel comfortable with that. They know how to take care of a house and yard. They pay the rent because it's such a discount compared to what they were paying which was probably somewhere between $1,200 and $1,400 a month. Now, they only have to spend $600 - $800 a month in rent. That's a great deal and very affordable for them. There's a big market for that.

Here's an example of a single-family purchase with renting as the exit strategy. The purchase price is $70,000. The estimated price discount is about $230,000 from where it was at the height of the market. Rehab costs are built in. The total out-of-pocket expense is

$70,000. The estimated gross rental for a property like this is about $9,600 a year. The property management fee is typically about 10 percent and the estimated taxes and insurance are around $1,500. Total estimated net rental income is around $7,000 per year. That's not a bad day. Even better, if the properties go up in value later on down the road, you're able to then go ahead and benefit both ways – from the rental income now and the increase in value later.

Single Family Home Purchase and Rent Example:	
Example Purchase Price:	$ 70,000
Estimated Price Discount*: (based on original sales price)	$230,000
Example Estimated Rehab Costs:	Included
Total Out-of-Pocket Expense:	$70,000
Estimated Gross Rental Income: (based on $800/month)	$9,600
Property Management Fee (10%):	$960
Estimated Taxes and Insurance:	$1,500
Estimated Net Rental Income:	$7,140

The vacancy rate right now is 5 percent which is the lowest vacancy rate for property rentals that southwest Florida has seen in quite some time. That means that the experts in the office are able to get properties rented quickly, sometimes within a week or two weeks. That's pretty fast. That gets the income started quickly. It gets the machine rolling.

Duplex Strategy

One of the benefits of duplexes is that you make more money because you're getting more per square foot. You might get $600 or $700 per side, or $1,200 - $1,400 a month from a duplex as opposed to $800 from a single family home. When you get done with the management fee and other miscellaneous expenses, you are netting about $1,000 per month per duplex. That's a high return on your money compared to all the other choices out there and you have a secure asset. It is a brilliant idea.

We use a lot of the same criteria when we look at duplexes as we do with single family houses. These duplexes need the same minimal work that we do on our single family properties, meaning paint, tile, carpet, appliances -- all simple things that are easily fixed within a couple of weeks or maybe three or four weeks at the most. It's easy to whip out the rehab, get the property on the market right away and get the numbers crunching so we can hit start getting a return on our investment as quickly as possible.

Here's a multifamily home cash purchase example. You put up $90,000 for a particular duplex and the discount is around $235,000 off what they were selling for at the all-time high. The rehab costs are included. Total out-of-pocket expense is $90,000. The gross rental income is right around $16,800. Management fee, 10 percent, or about $1,680. Estimated taxes and insurance are about $2,500, and the net rental income is around $12,600 per year. Now that's awesome. That's making some money. Just think if you had several of those, and just think if that was all done tax-free in a Roth IRA. That's the whole point. This has to be done in the Roth IRA to be able to obtain the kind of real wealth that you and I are talking about.

Multi-Family Home Cash Purchase Example	
Example Purchase Price:	$90,000
Estimated Price Discount*: (based on original sales price)	$235,000
Example Estimated Rehab Costs:	Included
Total Out-of-Pocket Expense:	**$90,000**
Estimated Gross Rental Income: (based on $1,400/month)	$16,800
Property Management Fee (10%):	$1,680
Estimated Taxes and Insurance:	$2,500
Estimated Net Rental Income:	**$12,620**

The chart on the following page shows you the Days On Market as well as the turnaround time. This has been over the last couple of years. Just reading down the DOM column, you can see that we are selling properties quickly. You get the idea; this is pretty short-term. Now, the average profit of this track record is around $25,000 or $26,000 a house. But what if the return was less than that? Let's say it was a $20,000 profit. Now, on $20,000 profit, if you made 40 percent of $20,000 profit, that's $8,000. Now, an $8,000 profit on $60,000 is a phenomenal return on your money.

	DATE ACQUIRED	PRICE	DATE SOLD	PRICE	GROSS PROFIT	% ROI	DOM	SQ FT	$/SF SELL	$/SF BUY	SPREAD	ROUND-TURN DAYS (CASH TO CASH)
1	10/17/2008	72050	1/21/2009	97000	24,950	35%	44	1594	61	45	16	95
2	11/6/2008	79100	3/5/2009	125800	46,700	59%	21	1936	66	41	25	119
3	11/26/2008	50750	1/23/2009	106150	57,400	113%	22	1619	71	31	40	57
4	11/26/2008	68050	1/6/2009	108150	40,100	59%	12	2035	53	33	20	41
5	12/12/2008	85400	12/30/2008	112000	26,600	31%	9	1969	57	43	14	18
6	12/16/2008	51000	3/19/2009	82000	31,000	61%	44	1583	51.81	32.21	19.61	93
7	12/31/2008	60000	2/20/2009	110000	50,000	83%	4	1797	61.21	33.38	27.83	52
8	12/31/2008	90150	4/17/2009	124000	33,850	38%	12	1936	67	47	20	107
9	1/13/2009	89000	2/24/2009	138000	49,000	55%	13	2012	68.59	44.23	24.36	41
10	1/21/2009	97000	3/31/2009	142900	45,900	47%	25	2359	60.58	41.11	17.47	69
11	1/21/2009	85000	3/19/2009	99000	14,000	52%	50	1796	55.06	36.15	18.91	57

12	1/22/2009	52100	4/2/2009	88000	35,900	69%	22	1610	55.84	32.36	23.48	70
13	1/22/2009	46200	3/13/2009	69000	22,800	49%	47	1528	45.16	30.23	14.93	50
14	1/28/2009	95700	5/21/2009	129500	33,800	35%	63	1993	64.97	48.01	16.96	114
15	1/28/2009	90050	6/10/2009	128000	37,950	42%	96	2017	63.46	44.64	18.82	132
16	2/4/2009	73200	4/1/2009	109900	36,700	50%	19	2015	54.54	36.32	18.22	55
17	2/4/2009	82100	4/8/2009	125000	42,900	52%	51	2421	51.63	33.91	17.72	62
18	2/12/2009	99550	4/24/2009	179000	79,450	80%	55	2232	80.19	44.61	35.58	70
19	2/16/2009	72950	4/2/2009	119000	46,050	63%	31	2004	59.38	36.41	22.97	44
20	3/10/2009	100500	4/28/2009	165000	64,500	64%	2	2209	74.69	45.48	29.21	48
21	3/10/2009	88000	6/9/2009	130000	42,000	48%	41	2044	63.61	43.05	20.55	89
22	3/12/2009	55100	7/2/2009	155000	99,900	181%	3	2019	76.77	27.29	49.48	110
23	3/12/2009	55300	4/24/2009	107000	51,700	93%	7	1822	58.73	30.35	28.38	42
24	3/19/2009	53000	4/8/2009	78000	25,000	47%	2	1455	53.61	36.42	17.19	19
25	3/19/2009	73500	8/21/2009	129900	56,400	77%	45	2097	61.94	35.05	26.89	148
26	3/25/2009	93500	5/15/2009	162500	69,000	74%	4	2040	79.66	45.83	33.83	50
27	4/14/2009	6600	7/7/2009	99900	93,300	51%	15	1425	70.12	46.31	23.81	83

28	4/17/2009	82500	7/2/2009	121000	38,500	47%	45	2050	59.02	40.24	18.78	75
29	4/22/2009	86000	7/17/2009	139000	53,000	62%	5	2324	59.81	37.05	22.76	85
30	4/22/2009	85500	6/24/2009	130000	44,500	52%	39	2335	55.67	36.61	19.06	62
31	4/17/2009	77400	7/1/2009	139000	61,600	79%	19	1421	97.81	54.46	43.35	74
32	4/30/2009	65000	7/20/2009	89000	24,000	37%	14	1408	63.21	48.16	17.05	80
33	5/4/2009	60000	8/6/2009	87000	27,000	45%	17	1458	59.67	41.15	18.52	92
34	4/17/2009	110350	7/10/2009	210000	99,650	90%	1	2681	78.32	41.16	37.16	83
35	4/29/2009	123000	7/10/2009	194000	71,000	58%	64	2009	95.56	61.22	35.34	71
36	4/16/2009	133000	8/15/2009	190000	57,000	43%	47	2237	84.93	59.45	25.48	119
37	5/28/2009	87000	8/21/2009	127000	40,000	48%	40	2199	57.75	39.56	18.19	83

You're looking at more than a 10% return, and that's my goal. I want to make sure that we're beating mutual funds, we're beating stocks, we're beating CDs, of course, and bonds and any of those other investments. The main goal is to try to find niche turnkey systems like this one that are done for you. Quite frankly, if you're one of those people that has to go ahead and do everything yourself, the actual results are going to be ten times slower. You have to empower other people to help you get your goals accomplished. You cannot possibly be a superhero.

Instead of trying to do it all yourself, use a team. Teams are the only way to go. Looking for houses, talking to sellers, rehabbing, it's all time-consuming. More than that, it's unnecessary and it costs you thousands of dollars of wasted time by not being able to go ahead and do something else. If you are able to invest your money and get a piece of the action and do more deals because you have a team in place that does it faster, you are far better off rather than trying to make the whole amount on your own. That's crazy. It is much better to partner on five deals a month than trying to do maybe one a month on your own. There's a big difference and we're talking big, big dollars. If you are an investor, stop wasting time looking for houses. That takes up your time day and night. It's a pain in the neck and unnecessary. Our turnkey systems already have the inventory.

How the Process Works

Our team calls the bank and says, "We need to look at five houses. What do you have?" The bank gives us seven days to look at the deal, go inspect it, and out of the five houses that we look at, maybe we will want to keep three of them. Then, we call you and let you know we've got a prospective property. You can take a look, kick the tires, see if it's something you want to participate in. By using a turnkey system, you can go back to doing what you enjoy, whether it's traveling or working, rather than waste time doing it yourself. The turnkey system will get you there quicker.

Best of all, this is definitely passive because you're not touching anything yourself and it can go into your Roth IRA tax-free. Just imagine if you use a Roth IRA to do this. Your Roth IRA benefits from having a profit every 120 days. Imagine how fast that money can compound. You can use it to buy more properties, maybe land. Maybe you make $10,000 profit, and you buy more land with that money. That works, and it is light years better than just leaving your money sitting there.

What are you going to do with that extra time? Well, rather than getting hot, dirty and sweaty rehabbing, why not find investors for multiple properties? Let's say you only have money for one house. How do you find more funds for other houses? You need to start looking for partners. Find out who could potentially partner with you, especially if they have an IRA. Do they have an old 401(k) plan? You'll find that investors will partner with you, and you still are in the deal even if you put no money in. Can you be 10-percent owner of a deal if you brought all the money to the table? Absolutely. That would work. Why wouldn't an investor make you partner for putting the deal together to make them money?

Now, one of the reasons not everyone does this is because they don't have direct access to the banks. Remember, the bank doesn't want to just talk to anybody. They want to talk to someone who's in the business of buying and selling homes, someone with a provable track record. They want to talk to someone who really can close on the houses in seven days and not miss the closing or skip a day. You know what I mean. They're looking for someone who's credible, reliable and can pay cash and come to closing in seven days. Those are the people that they tend to give the deals to. They don't just give it to anybody who calls in off the street.

Bank-owned properties need work, and not everybody wants to get involved with trying to find out what the best prices are and who is going to do the best work and not screw it up and create more damage. These are the things that will eat up your time and cause massive frustration for most people. In addition, most of the bank-owned properties that you know of in your town probably are not nearly new. One of the reasons why I like southwest Florida, in particular this location in Lee County, is because of the fact that the houses are nearly new. I like it when the customer feels that the house is new and that it's not going to have maintenance problems any time soon. That takes half of the fear out of buying a property.

When a buyer sees a house that's crisp and is only a couple of years old, they feel like that they don't have to worry about the roof. They don't have to worry about the air conditioner. They don't have to worry about the normal things that deteriorate on a property. The house has a long life, and in some cases, there's even a warranty still in place. You never know what you're going to find and there are some real gems in there.

Turnkey Out of the Box Investment Secret Number Two is a wholesale and refurbishing system with a proven track record and the most cost-effective method to make exponential returns on your investment. It's done for you. It's automatic. You don't have to get involved with anything. Let the experts do their job. They know what to fix, how to get the rehab done fast, how to get it on the market and what price to price it at. They definitely have a feel for this.

We can't second-guess the experts. We have the best team assembled to work with you. These people who are partners of mine are experts at really getting the job done, getting the house bought, fixed and sold and getting your money turned so that you can invest over and over and over again, while the train is rolling. The time to get started is now.

TURNKEY INVESTMENT SECRET STRATEGY #3

ASSET-BASED LENDING

T urnkey Out of the Box Investment Secret Number Three is Asset-Based Lending. This particular investment is a little bit different from what we've been talking about in that it is non-real estate related. This is a strong way to diversify your portfolio to other things besides houses and land.

Asset-Based lending is a passive money-making investment secret that not many people are privy to. Most everyone knows about stocks, bonds and mutual funds but most people have not even heard of asset-based lending, much less understand it. Only a select few probably use it. Since it is non-real estate related, it's definitely going to provide you with a way to spread out your risk. It gives you some of the diversification you need to minimize the downside of investing in only one industry.

The Problem is the Opportunity

When there's a problem in the market there's always opportunity. We want to take advantage of the right market at the right time and this is the perfect time for asset-based lending. Here's the problem that exists: Lines of credit are not available for creditworthy companies. Banks are not loaning money, not even temporary or short-term lines of credit for inventory for good, credit-worthy companies. That creates a problem that we can solve and benefit from. Businesses that normally get approved for loans are having problems getting any kind of money for manufacturing, for buying inventory and other normal business financing from conventional lenders.

The opportunity for profit always exists when we can solve a problem. The solution to this particular problem is asset-based lending -- giving profitable companies the financing they need. They pledge their cashable assets as collateral. Typically, companies use their inventory or their accounts receivable as collateral to secure the loan. This collateral helps protect us in the event of default. In fact, because we over-collateralize the loans, it actually is a deterrent to default.

Just so you know, this is not factoring. Factoring is where a business sells its accounts receivables at a discount. The factor is assigned the receivables and the money is paid straight to the factoring company. In asset-based lending, companies can pledge their accounts receivables as part or all of the collateral, however, the accounts receivable are only taken in the case of borrower default. Asset-Based lending is a business loan that is collateralized by inventory, property or accounts receivables.

Our Borrower Profile

Obviously, we don't take on bad companies. We work only with solid companies and we help them to do better. There are high-qualifying requirements. First of all, the companies we work with are what we call "Bank-Qualified" -- most of these businesses would be approved by banks if the banks had the ability or desire to loan money.

In addition, the companies pledge Cashable Collateral. The asset-based lending program takes 125 percent to as much as 200 percent of the loan amount in presold inventory and accounts receivable. For example, if a company wanted to borrow $75,000, we might require $100,000 to $150,000 in inventory or accounts receivable. This over-collateralization gives the borrower a strong incentive to repay the loan and helps protect us from a default.

Third, borrowers typically have a high monthly profit margin. When a borrower is making money monthly from selling their product, whatever it may be, their profit is usually between 20 to 25 percent per month. They are willing to pay four percent to five percent a month for a private loan. That's where we come in.

Loan amounts are generally under $250,000. More typically, they are in the $50,000 - $150,000 range. That is what we target. We are not financing start-up companies. We are not financing businesses that are so small that $150,000 will pay all their expenses for a year. We deal only with companies that have established track records, who can prove revenues and who are not relying on this loan to finance their entire operation.

Loans are typically made for revenue-generation: Inventory financing, expansion capital, cash-flow bridging. We do not bail out failing companies. But businesses need working capital. They need lines of credit and they sometimes need a bridge to help them over temporary shortfalls.

Asset-based loans are short-term. The beauty of this is that the amount of time between payout and pay back is short enough that you can see a fast return on your money, take the profit and reinvest again. Your money is not swinging in the wind for five or ten years.

At one point, asset-based lending was known as the "loan of last resort." Now it is a viable method of freeing up cash that may be tied up in inventory, receivables or equipment. The assets are in place and quantified; they just are not as liquid as a business may need them to be.

Here are two examples of the kinds of companies that would get a loan of this type:

- A sign manufacturing company needs $46,000. They give us $100,000 in collateral, which would be accounts receivable or inventory or both. The collateralized amount is 215% in this case. Their annual revenues are $4 million, so we know that we can easily collect the loan amount from the revenues alone that are coming in monthly.

- Software company: Loan amount, $121,000. They gave us $500,000 in collateral. This works out to 410% collateral on the money. This company does $2 million a year in revenues.

As you can see, these are good companies with solid cash flow. Pet supplies, software, home improvement, etc., there are many good companies out there that need short-term financing. All of them have good collateral.

Benefits

Investors like us can invest in private placement loans to these companies and we can make four to five percent a month for private loans. The investors receive a portion of that, which comes out to between 25 to 35 percent a year. To make 25% a year on your money compared to what our other choices are is absolutely phenomenal. And if you are using funds from your Roth IRA and making these profits tax free, that's even better.

Now, the benefit to investors is they make approximately 27% a year on their money. The distributions are made quarterly which is a 6.75 percent return on investment quarterly. Let's say you invested $50,000. The first quarter you would make $3,375. It's the same, of course, with the other three quarters as well. You would end up with $3,375 every quarter which comes out to a $13,500 profit in one year. That's been typical for one after another after another of these investments with over 30 of these successfully completed.

Risks

There's always risk in getting any return, especially 27 percent a year. What are the risks? The first risk is that the loan payment is late or delayed. That's a minor risk but more of a bump in the road than an insurmountable problem. If, in fact, the customer asks for an extension, we will extend it to 18 months and the distributions will continue just as such. If that's the case, you still keep getting paid even if it's longer than one year. But it is also a reason why we look for companies with a strong cash flow. The stronger the cash flow, the less likely a company is to be late or unable to make its payment.

The second risk is that the client defaults on the loan. That could possibly happen.

Let's say, for example, that a client doesn't pay and we're not able to recover it from the monthly revenues. The company has pledged inventory which is in our name until they pay for it, i.e., repay the loan. We have the right and ability to sell that inventory to a competitor or some other outlet. And, because we have over-collateralized the loan, we can sell that inventory at a discount for a faster sale. The collateralization is another way to protect your downside. That seems to me that with that much collateral, it brings your risk down significantly compared to if you had no other collateral or just monthly revenues to protect yourself on the downside.

Our Partner Criteria

Experience is a large part of success in any investment strategy and we partner with some of the most experienced, well-versed names in the Asset-Based Lending Industry. Lenders in this field need to have a strong analytical background as well as an in-depth knowledge of various industries and the companies within those industries.

Asset-based lending is a wide field. Each lender specializes in various industries, loan amounts, lending parameters, even geographical areas. There are large commercial asset-based lenders such as Wells Fargo, Goldman Sachs and Citigroup as well as regional lenders such as Regions Bank and Bank West. But asset-based loans from these commercial entities have dried up except to a few incredibly large (and largely government-guaranteed) corporations.

Small to medium size businesses are left out in the cold. Certain industries can't get the time of day from banks right now. Yet they are still doing business, day in and day out.

Market Reach

Partnering with established companies allows us to leverage not only their expertise, but to capitalize on their market reach. We look for lenders who are well-known in the industries that fit into our lending criteria.

We have partnered with asset-based lenders who specialize in small business lending and who are known in certain particular fields. We look for industry leaders who have become the "go-to" lender and we leverage their client base. They know who the players are, they can tell hich business is going to make it and which one isn't. They know what margins each business should be operating at. This last point is key.

The most important component of any lending program (at least from the viewpoint of the lender) is the borrower's ability to repay the debt. Our partners are able to analyze a company's financial statements and know immediately if their revenues are where they should be. Quite frankly, if a company's revenues aren't enough to pay back the loan, they don't make the cut. Our partners have the depth of experience necessary to minimize our risk of ever having to take back collateral.

Another important benefit of our partners' market reach in various industries is that if a borrower did default and they had to take back the collateral, they have a built-in list of buyers for that collateral from their previous dealings within the industry.

To recap, we partner with companies who have a minimum of over a decade of experience, who consistently show returns in the 25% - 35% range and who have strong relationships with and a deep knowledge of the industries in which they lend.

Could you do asset-based lending on your own? Possibly. If you had a deep knowledge of market conditions in the area, demand for product, were able to analyze company financials, could ascertain the margins on each business and know how those margins compare with industry standards, knew companies within the industry, knew the price of goods and equipment and, of course, had the time to do it all.

Frankly, I don't have that kind of time. And if I did, I sure don't want to spend it pouring over spreadsheets and crunching numbers. Wealth isn't built by you working. Wealth is built by making your money work.

One reason why we partner with many different companies for our various investment strategies is that no one is able to know everything about everything. We partner with people who know their industries, who work in it every day and have decades of knowledge to back them up. We leverage their expertise so that we don't have to do the work. That's investing.

Why is this investment good? We are always talking about getting passive income. As we mentioned before, passive investments are going to come in quarterly, monthly, weekly or whatever the set period is. This investment is 100 percent passive and the risk is minimal with secured collateral.

The high preferential rate of return out performs most real estate transactions and mutual funds. Returns in the area of 20 to 27 percent, even 30 percent, are beating mutual funds, stocks, bonds, CDs, etc. That's why you have to take a close look at this and get your hands around it and understand it.

If you are stuck in mutual funds or you're stuck in stocks or even in your IRA, this is a great way to transfer out of that and put that money into something that might work faster. It would take years to get rich in mutual funds and stocks. There's not enough time in your lifetime or my lifetime to accumulate the money we need from those investments. Most of us don't have that kind of time.

Think about it. Don't just nod your head. You've got to ask yourself, what is the likelihood of getting rich the old way, with stocks and mutual funds? It's very difficult because you can't even leverage your own efforts as you can with real estate. Asset-based lending is one way to diversify and with its strong cash flow, to start to get back what you've lost in your portfolios if you've already had some bad times.

Asset-Based Lending From Your Roth IRA

Why use your self-directed Roth IRA to do asset-based lending? Obviously, a 27 percent return is rockin'. Do you really want the government cutting your return in half? It's still a good return compared to many investments. However, using your Roth IRA will get you those returns tax-free. The cumulative effect of tax-free returns and reinvestment will build your wealth ten times faster than doing the same investment outside your IRA.

Join the Team

Once you join our asset-based lending program, you are now part of the network. Because of that, you get first right of refusal as each individual program is introduced. Any time a new opportunity comes out, you have first choice before it goes out to new members. I want to make sure that you understand that you are at the top of the list.

Asset-based lending is exciting in so many ways. Yes, the returns are fantastic. But more importantly, the timing is right and the need for this service is strong. Again, every problem presents an opportunity. The tight lending atmosphere from conventional lenders is stifling the growth of stable, successful companies. Asset-based lending provides needed capital to working businesses while providing strong returns to the investor. That's a win/win in any book.

TURNKEY INVESTMENT SECRET STRATEGY #4

OIL AND GAS

Turnkey Out of the Box Investment Secret Number Four is one of the investments that I like the most because it happens to be the most aggressive. We are going discuss how to invest in oil and gas projects: How to do it right and what to look for.

This is all information that we have studied for quite some time and I want to pass onto you. I have learned many secrets about how to invest in oil and gas and exactly what to look for. I'm going to give you an example of an oil and gas project that we and our students are investing in. I'm going to show you exactly what type of a program that we invest in and why, so you get the idea of how this investment works and how it can benefit you.

This will help you to determine how to measure risk and reward when investing in similar oil and gas projects. I'm going to cover one of our existing oil and gas projects in a general sense to see if it will help you understand what makes one oil and gas drilling program safer than another and what makes one oil and gas drilling program more profitable than another, as well.

This is not your typical oil and gas drilling program; in fact, it is quite unique. There are some things that are different about this investment strategy that you're going to find that make this completely different from all other strategies that you've seen before.

This is a niche market. As you know, fuel and alternative fuels are a big topic right now and oil drilled in the United States on land is extremely valuable.

Number one, the price of oil will probably continue to go up over the next several years, so we probably have a good chance to benefit from any oil drilling in the United States that is not offshore. For this particular case, we're going to show you a drilling program that is onshore and not in the middle of the ocean, which involves a higher risk factor.

Investing in oil and gas is typically reserved for wealthy people who can afford to take more risk with a portion of their portfolio. Higher risk often includes a greater chance of a higher return and people can become quite wealthy from putting money into a program that might be considered exotic or high risk, but has a proven success track record. Again this is definitely different from anything you've ever heard of, and I'm going to go through the pros and cons and all of the pluses about using this type of a program compared to the others you may be familiar with.

Now, all my professional life I've had oil and gas programs cross my desk to look at, and most of the time they were either not successful or they were not very profitable because they were structured incorrectly or I didn't feel comfortable with the investor payout arrangement.

Let me give you an example. Most oil and gas drilling programs are set up where they have you invest money, you drill for wells and you're wildcatting, which means that you're just guessing and going out and drilling holes in the ground where you think there might be oil.

Unfortunately, that's the riskiest scenario of all. Wildcatting is where the drilling company is just drilling in different places hoping to find oil when there is no proven oil there. I only invest in oil drilling programs that have existing oil wells that are currently producing. In other words, I'm looking for something where I know there's oil nearby, where if I drill not that far from the first well than I should be able to hit oil on the second well, third well, fourth well, etc.

One of the things that greatly reduces the risk from our investment strategy is that we are definitely not wildcatting. We are very particular about the drilling companies that we work with; we look for solid businessmen, not starry-eyed dreamers who want us to finance their oil adventure. Wildcatting is not for us. We work with companies that go where the oil is. They choose areas where oil has already been found and has proved its production capabilities.

Because oil production is such a highly regulated industry, we are able to keep an eye on what is going on in the oil fields, from the comfort of our laptops. Well production is audited and you can actually track the production online including how many and which wells have been drilled and the number of barrels pumped.

I like the ability to see what is coming out of the ground right now. It helps me feel more comfortable with this investment. If I were able to drill near those particular wells that are already producing, my chances of hitting new wells and making money are a heck of a lot greater. That just makes sense.

Our Investment Strategy

This is a private placement program and in this particular drilling program, we are drilling for 15 wells. Remember a private placement is an investment that you put money into along with other people. The money is used to drill in a specific area that is listed in the private placement documents. In other words, there's no guessing. They actually have to go ahead and drill exactly where they tell you they're going to drill, on the acreage that they have leased.

In most oil and gas drilling programs that I have looked at, I have seen that as an investor I don't get paid until all of the expenses are paid -- drilling the wells, any other administrative expenses, paying the people who are running the program. As an investor I would get paid last.

This private placement is set up completely different, and you probably have never seen this structure before. This particular structure is set up more securely in that we get paid first. The investors like you and I get paid off the top as a royalty investor, as a royalty owner. We become partners with the drilling company. If we're partners with the drilling company and the drilling company gets paid for drilling the well, we get paid first off the top for profits. We are in the driver's seat.

And that means that we don't have to wait until all the expenses are paid before we get paid. We get paid every single month and that's another very good point. All of the oil drilling programs that I have seen have stated that you, the investor, get paid at the end of a year or two. That's a long time to wait for your original investment to come back and to get your return. We are able to structure a different and definitely more advantageous payout.

This private placement is set up so we get paid monthly from the first month a drilling company starts hitting oil. If oil is hit tomorrow, next month the money from the sale of the oil goes right to the accounting department and then the accounting department sends us a check as a royalty interest owner. I like that. I like a monthly or quarterly return on my investments if I can get that.

The other thing that's different about this particular program is that this private placement puts you in a partnership position with the drilling companies. Rather than pay a drilling company up front and have to worry about them not hitting oil, we have it set up so that the drilling company does not get paid any profit unless they hit oil.

So the original drilling costs are covered, but the actual profit that the oil drilling company would make doesn't come to them **until** they hit oil, and **after** the investors are paid. If they hit oil today, then the profit that the oil drilling company would make would come after you and I as investors have already been paid.

There are several positive things going on here. Just to recap: Number one is that we are partners with the drilling companies, unlike other programs where we have to pay them profits whether we hit oil or not. That's a huge plus for me. I like that because now I feel like a drilling company is going to do its best to hit oil.

The second thing I want to recap is that the payout to you and me is made on a monthly basis. Instead of having to wait a year or two or worse, three or four to see if we get any return, we will receive monthly checks.

Now, the projected return on this is quite high. We're going to drill 15 wells in each one of these programs. Out of those 15 wells, we have projected that 10 wells will yield oil. In this scenario, the return on our money could be as high as 8, 9 or 10 percent a month.

And yes, that's a month. I'm saying to you that if you can hit X amount of barrels at X amount of price with 10 wells, which I'll show you in the next few pages, your projected return should be roughly between 8 and 10 percent per month. That's a lot. That means that you're almost doubling your money every year. And yes, of course, it's very aggressive. But we have reduced most of the risk by drilling next to existing wells. Also, there's the advantage of having a royalty partner owner interest rather than having to wait until all the expenses are paid to see if there's anything left for you and me. Those are all things that could make this investment not only lucrative but much safer than other drilling programs.

Remember, I always tell you that it's critical to measure your downside risk. That is, how much can I lose? The only way that I could lose my money in this strategy would be if they drilled 15 wells and didn't hit any oil at all. Literally, they would have to drill all 15 wells and not hit any oil at all for me to be at risk. If they hit one or two wells out 15, I still can make my money back and more.

We'll go over some of that in the next few pages. I want to go ahead and just make sure you at least get the highlights and the summary of why this is so powerful. As you can probably tell, I am very excited about this particular oil drilling program. It truly is unlike any other.

Our Partner – The Drilling Company

Before entering into any investment, I need to feel very comfortable with the people and the companies that I will be dealing with. There are actually two parties that we are working with: The private placement company and the actual drilling company. Even though private placements are strictly regulated, it is still important to me that I know the people behind the private placement and that I feel comfortable with their level of expertise as well as integrity. My many years in the industry have afforded me the opportunity to meet and observe many of the "players" in the private placement field. All those years have paid off and I am proud to say that the private placement companies we work with are truly top notch.

We look for drilling companies with strong track records. Our optimal company has over 20 years in the drilling business and has a track record that is public and transparent. We want to see an established company, with a solid foundation and strong monthly cash flow. We don't want to prop up a fading company. We look for companies that are positioned to expand their operations and have the equipment and personnel in place to move quickly. That's powerful.

The drilling companies that we work with drill based on geological reports, which is different from what you may have seen before. A lot of drilling companies don't use geological reports to decide where they should drill. A geological report, if it's done right, can show you specifically where all the pockets of gas and oil are, which gives you a much better chance of hitting oil. You're not just guessing.

Number one, we're drilling next to existing wells. Number two is that we're using geological reports to pick the exact spot to drill. I'll show you in just a few pages what the geological reports look like. This is all very easy to verify and very easy to find out and prove.

Let's go forward and let me show you some more secrets here.

The first step is for the company to secure exclusive drilling and mineral rights to a tract of land, usually hundreds of acres, in the United States, not offshore. It's onshore and more importantly, they will lease land where there is proven oil production in the area already. You can easily check all the stuff out online and see how many barrels are pumping. It's all very current and all information is verifiable and regulated.

This is a turnkey oil drilling program. It's a private placement where all of us put our money together to pay for the drilling of 15 wells. Then we sit back and let the drilling company do its job. We're expecting to drill 15 wells with an estimated yearly return of $4.4 million per year.

If we were able to drill 15 wells, and even if we didn't hit oil on all of those, we're expecting to hit $4.4 million in revenues per year. Now, these projections, as you know, are based on geological reports, past history and past production of wells right there, and current oil production that has been furnished to us by the operators.

The drilling company will furnish us with the current oil production from this exact location, so we can see how many barrels per day are pumped. We can see exactly what price the refinery is paying for each barrel of oil. In this case we have very strong data that shows that there is already oil there and that the geology reports are showing that there are definitely, definitely other pockets of oil right near the ones that we've currently drilled.

On the following page is an aerial photograph of one of our actual properties. The outlined section is the property, which is 417 acres. That's a good-sized piece of land. We can drill a lot of wells on this property. The plan is to drill 85 wells in the next couple of years, but we're only doing one set of 15 at a time. Our goal is to hit seven, eight, nine, 10 wells out of 15. It's very, very probable that we will. We're going to do approximately six private placements, which is six different investments of 15 wells each private placement.

The dark spots in the above photo are from a geological report showing gas content and the geochemical analysis of specifically where all the pockets of gas are. You will typically find the oil is underneath the pockets of gas.

We know that these particular pockets of gas are the best spots to drill. In this example, there are currently five wells on the property that are producing right now. We'll drill near all of those wells and in the pockets of gas. We actually drill down below the gas to go ahead and pull up the oil.

This is all sweet crude oil, meaning the best quality of oil that we can find, that is currently being pumped out of there.

We will drill 15 wells all at one time, so that within 30 to 60 days we will have completed all of our drilling and then we will know exactly how many out of the fifteen have hit oil. That's pretty exciting. Again, if we just hit one out of 15 we'll be happy. It's still a very good return, but if we were able to hit five or seven or eight or 10 wells out of 15, the money will flow.

We also have seven approved and permitted future drilling locations as well. Even after we finish and complete these particular wells we have seven other approved areas for future drilling that could be potentially ongoing for us.

Projections

I want to show you the project's core foundation, and explain to you exactly how we established our projections on the potential of this investment.

Our baseline is what we think might happen based on very conservative estimates. The first number we looked at was the ADP or Average Daily Oil Well Production. We're expecting that we're going to pump 65 barrels a day based on past performance.

Now there are many wells that can produce more than 65 barrels a day, like 70, 80, 90 or 100 even barrels per day, but we're going to use 65 as our baseline as an example of what we feel are the most conservative estimates of what could happen with this particular program. We're saying that we expect to hit at least 65 barrels per day per well, and again there are wells producing 100 barrels a day, so we feel very comfortable with that number.

Our second baseline factor is the ACR, or Average Oil Drilling Conversion Rate. We're expecting that 70 percent of the wells that we drill will hit oil. Out of 15 wells, that's 10 wells. Again, this is based on past performance.

It's important that you know that this is not a guess. The drilling companies that we use have been able to hit 70 percent of all the wells they've ever drilled. That is where experience pays off and that is one component of the track record we look at when we evaluate our drilling companies. Again, out of 15 wells we expect to hit 10 wells producing oil. That's very good. And again, if we only hit five wells or three wells, it's still a phenomenal percentage rate return on our money. We're going to use 70 percent based on past performance of the conversion rate as our baseline.

The third factor is the sales price per barrel. We're saying that conservatively, we expect to get $75 a barrel. Now, I don't know if any of you are following the current market, but oil has hit $90 a barrel and has topped $100 a barrel. If we are able to get $90 per barrel, the numbers that we have projected conservatively would be significantly higher.

But in this case we're going to use the conservative number of $75 a barrel. We're going to expect to hit 10 wells out of 15, and we're going to use 65 barrels per day per well as our baseline. This is just our baseline on what we think would happen. Now, when I go forward and show you the projections and show you what type of return could potentially happen here you'll understand just how conservative our numbers are and that returns could be much greater or somewhat short of that.

The Opportunity

The program, which again, is a private placement, represents an attractive investment opportunity for the following reasons:

1. **Track Record**. The operators we work with have tons of experience and they've been doing this, as I said, for over 20 years. The experience of the drillers was important to me and I want to be certain that I've got someone who knows what they're doing, can get the wells drilled quickly and has a track record of hitting 70 percent of the wells they drill.

That's a very good track record to have in a partner. They have established, completed and maintained many different investment programs where they were able to complete the drilling and hit seven out of 10 wells. I have a good comfort level with this and it makes me feel good that the operator has a track record that other drillers have not been able to prove.

2. **Selective Drilling**. The companies we use have developed a highly selective approach to investing in drilling and exploration projects based on rigorous technical analysis. Again, they're using geological reports. They've used careful risk assessment and financial analysis of risk-adjusted returns.

3. **The Royalty Interest** is as follows: The program has secured an overriding royalty interest, which means, as I mentioned to you earlier, that you would be a royalty interest owner, which produces an income based on total growth revenues.

That's important because we're not going to get paid out of net revenues. We're getting paid off the gross, which is obviously, better. We don't have to wait until expenses are all spent and then get paid; you and I get paid as a partner in this deal off the top. That's never been done before that I know of.

I've looked at tons and tons of projects just like this, and I've never seen it where we as investors can get paid from drilling a well off the top before all expenses. That's phenomenal. The interest that we have in this investment is free of all associated operational costs and business expenses. There are no expenses whatsoever that come ahead of you and I getting our return on our money.

That makes sense to me because we're taking all the risk with our money, aren't we? We're putting up all the money therefore we should be paid first before all expenses.

4. Cost Limits. The program will invest into 15 oil wells and maintain a cost limit on the investment capital per well, so we know ahead of time what it's going to cost us to drill per well.

In other words, the drilling company has given us a price and that is the price that they have to stick to. If it costs more money to drill that well, they have to eat that. Once we have established what the cost of a well will be, we don't have to worry about it running higher than that because we don't have to pay for it. The drilling company is responsible for paying any costs above and beyond the drilling prices they have given us.

It's important to me that we don't have any surprises, no guessing, no things that will come that were unusual about the cost of drilling for this program.

5. Tax Considerations. Many people use their IRA or they will roll over an old 401(k) plan into a new self-directed IRA, probably a Roth, which is tax-free, and then use the funds from the IRA to invest in this project. For myself and all of my students, we are using IRAs to invest in this because when we make money monthly we want that money go into our account tax free.

Now, if you're not investing using an IRA you may qualify for a 50 percent depletion allowance tax benefit, and a 75 percent intangible drilling cost tax benefit. There are some tax benefits for you investing in this project, whether you use an IRA or not. You

Michael Poggi

should make sure that you let your accountant know about that so he can utilize those tax benefits for you at tax time.

6. Profit Distribution. The program will disburse all payments, all net profits, on a monthly basis. Every month you are paid right from the refinery, right from the accounting. The payment goes from sale to the refinery, right to the accountant and right to your bank account.

The Business Model

The program will consist of 80 units interest, of which 40 of them are for sale. In other words, you and I as investors have the ability to buy 40 of the 80 units that are available.

The 40 units are priced at a fixed amount per unit, which you and I can take advantage of either as full units, half a unit or a quarter of a unit, which I'll explain. We are offering these units to accredited investors only. The one-time capital investment of a quarter of a unit is just under $16,000. A half-unit is just under $32,000 and one full unit is $63,750.

These are the different areas of investments that you could pick for your IRA or using cash. Now, if you're interested in doing a larger share, of course, we would have larger shares available. Each private placement is approximately $2.5 million, just so you have a general idea of what we typically look for.

Here's a scenario. On a quarter-unit if we hit the projections that I showed you earlier using our baseline, then your return should be 95 percent per year. That's quite high, but again does it happen? Yes. There are definitely people who make money on oil drilling programs and make that kind of return, especially when you have it in your favor, where there are already existing oil wells and you're not wildcatting.

109

Take a look at the monthly return. You are paid monthly on this based on our conservative projections of 7.9 percent per month. And remember these are just estimates; returns range higher or lower than that. This is just to give you a general idea of projected typical returns based on our baseline.

The same thing applies for a half unit and, of course, the same thing applies for one full unit. In other words, a projected return is 95 percent per year. Whether we hit that or not, we'll know when we drill, but it could be even higher than that based on conservative estimates. But without trying it, without putting money at risk, you're never going to know -- you can't make money if you don't try it. You can't make money if you don't give it a whirl and invest in these types of things.

Now, here's one other thing that's important. When we say 95 percent per year, take a look at that. That's for the whole life of the well. How long do wells normally produce oil? Typically 10 to 15 years. That's based on a 10-well completion scenario based on 65 barrels a day for each well, and based on $75 a barrel. These are where the estimates are coming from. That's for 10 to 15 years. Let's say you invested $100,000 into one of these drilling programs, and let's say that we did hit those projections of 95 percent per year.

That means that you would see almost all your entire investment returned within one year. Better still, you would now basically double that investment every year for the next 15 years. That's the potential of this project, that's why it's so attractive. You get paid every year continuously until that oil well runs dry. Potentially that's between 10 and 15 years of payments on one investment where you had all your money returned within approximately 12 months. That sounds very exciting to me.

So, is it worth the risk? Absolutely. Now, how much should you risk in your portfolio depending on your age and your risk tolerance? Well, typically a person in their 40s or 50s should risk about 10 percent of their portfolio in this particular area, meaning higher risk but yet potentially very, very high return. It's definitely worth looking at.

Let's take a look now at what the actual plan is. The drilling completion time to drill all 15 wells is approximately one to two months. In 60 days the drilling company will go out and drill 15 wells and then we should know right away how many wells hit oil out of 15. Again, our projected number is 10 wells, that's a 70 percent conversion rate, which is a provable rate that they've been using all these years.

We're expecting to hit 10 wells out of 15. That's exciting. The cost to drill one well is $120,000. Now, once the well is drilled, if there is oil then the cost to take the oil out of the ground and get it to the refinery is $50,000 per well. Obviously, the drilling company does not get the other $50,000 to take the oil out of the ground if they don't hit oil. That is money saved. If there's no oil hit for that well, then we as investors will probably end up getting some money back because if we didn't hit oil, the cost to complete the well will not have been spent.

All we're paying for is the oil drilling, the completion money gets paid only if they hit oil. The total cost to drill a well and then take the oil out of the ground is $170,000. That's a fixed cost that the drilling company has to go ahead and abide by. We don't have to worry about any more expenses; that's all included already as fixed costs.

If we hit 10 wells, which is our completion scenario, and you invested $14,000 or 15,000, this is how much money you would actually have really spent. Instead of spending the full $16,000, you would have only spent $14,375 because we would have some money left over from the wells that did not hit. If we drill 15 wells and only hit 10 wells, then there's money left over that we will not have used that is returned to us. That's exciting as well.

Let's go over some investment highlights. We're expecting 65 barrels a day; total for all of the wells -- 650 barrels total per day.

That puts monthly production at 19,500 barrels. That works out to a total of 234,000 barrels for the year. That's awesome. Again, these are projected numbers based on our conservative baseline estimates from what we already know about the drilling companies' track records and typical oil production in the area.

There are 40 total units that are available for purchase by investors like you and I. The total profit for all those units per year is $2 million. We're expecting -- and this is an estimate -- $2 million per year in profits. The net profit is $54,000 per unit. That's how we come up with 95 percent return. If you invested $100,000 in this program you should be getting 95 percent return on your money, which is $95,000.

If you invest in a quarter-unit and we hit 10 wells out of 15, you would have invested a total of $14,375. The projected return on that is 95 percent, so you would end up with approximately $13,000 back at the end of 12 months, paid monthly. On $14,000 you'd have $13,000 return based on our conservative estimates.

That equals a return of 7.95 percent return per month, which is equivalent to $1,100 a month. And that can go into your Roth IRA tax free. Just imagine if you had 95 percent return come into your Roth IRA for the year and that was all done tax free. What does that mean to you and me? As investors if we bought this oil and gas program in our IRA, Roth, and it returned 95 percent return on our money on the year, what do we get to do with that money?

Do we owe any money to the government? No -- tax-free in a Roth IRA. That means that we could reinvest the total amount of money in other investments. Because none of our profits went to pay taxes, we are able to exponentially grow our wealth. This is a real goldmine when you use a Roth IRA.

The difference between doing this inside your IRA as opposed to outside of an IRA is astronomical. Think about how much more money we could keep because of not having to pay taxes on it. By doing this in a Roth IRA, we're going to get ahead way faster than if we did it outside of an IRA.

Now, remember the average lifespan of a producing oil well is 10 to 15 years. We could potentially make this kind of return that many years, 10 to 15 years. That is significant.

And that to me is worth taking a chance. When we're investing in something like this we're placing a bet. We're betting that we're going to hit 5, 10 or 11 wells out of 15 wells. That to me is a safe bet, since we already know there's oil there. They are already producing oil, the drillers have experience and we are a royalty interest owner getting paid off the top. It's worth it to do that.

Let's talk about the use of funds. I mentioned to you that the total cost of drilling is $120,000 per well. Fifteen wells times $120,000 per well is $1.8 million, which is the cost of the drilling for the wells.

If they hit oil, it is $50,000 to complete each well. If we were to hit 15 out of 15 wells, that would be phenomenal. But if we did it would also entail $750,000 in completion costs. The total capital raised for the 40 units is $2.5 million. The private placement that we're talking about here needs $2.5 million to complete the drilling of 15 wells, and that's where we come in as investors.

Now if you take the $2.5 million needed divided by the 40 units that are offered, one unit equals $63,750 per unit, which is how we came up with the unit price. If you were to invest $63,750 in one unit, you now own one out of 40 total units available.

Remember this: All the proceeds from this program investment offering are applied and used for drilling and completion of oil wells only. That means that none of this money, the 2.5 million dollars that we all invest into, is used for anybody's salaries or anything else. It's specifically used for drilling and completing the wells. Therefore, there are no other expenses that you would have to worry about at all -- no administration fees, no office staff, none of that stuff. Remember, the drilling company has their own expenses that they pay out of their own pocket from their profits.

You and I as investors are only paying for the well drilling. You and I only have to pay for drilling the well and getting the oil out of the ground over to the refinery. That limits our risk. No other oil programs are like this, not a one, and I've looked at probably 40 or 50 just in the last five or 10 years. I can tell you that none of them are structured this way.

The idea here is that the money is used to drill, not to pad someone else's pocket or to pay someone a salary while we're hoping we get oil drilled. I like this because of the reduction of risk and high potential for return. This to me makes total sense.

Here's how the profits get distributed to everyone. They drill the oil, they hit the oil, they take it out of the ground; it goes to the refinery. The refinery sends it over to the partnership, which has a CPA firm that will then take the funds and distribute them to the investors immediately. It goes from the oil well to the refinery, over to the partnership, to the accountants, and then right from the accountants back to your IRA or to you.

There is no other pathway. This is the fastest way for you and I to make our money -- by going right from the refinery to our pocket because we're getting paid off the gross revenues. As soon as the oil is drilled and sold we get paid immediately as a royalty owner, as a partner, not as an investor who gets paid way later after all kinds of expenses are paid out.

We get paid as a partner off the top. That's phenomenal. You won't find that payment structure anywhere.

Let me tell you some advantages now, why I feel this program is so powerful. From the beginning, here are the reasons why we should be doing this.

Benefits

Number one, we are royalty interest owners based on total growth revenues. That's never heard of before. That's phenomenal.

Number two, we get paid monthly, not at the end of a year or two or three, meaning they get to play with our money for years. We get paid right off the top, right in the beginning, monthly. The strong focus is on cash flow, meaning every single month getting cash flow for all of us.

Third, we have tax advantages. Using a Roth IRA has strong advantages. If it's not in your IRA you'll have other tax advantages and you should check with your tax accountant so that you can take advantage of those different tax benefits.

Fourth, you have full transparency, which is extremely important when you are investing your money. You, as a partner in this deal will see everything, such as how many oil wells hit, how many barrels per day they are producing, what the oil sells for per barrel. You will see all of the public reports that I will see. Everything is public knowledge and transparent, so you can track our progress and results, and see exactly what's going on.

Everything needs to be available and above board, so there are no hidden expenses, nothing is hidden from you, it's all fully transparent. Everyone will have access to this and remember it's highly regulated so there is no way that the numbers could be cheated or fudged. They are all very accurate and are audited and very highly regulated.

Again, all the oil production is available online, all the production reports are visible to us so we can see exactly what's going on and how our money is used and what the results are.

No additional capital is required to maintain this asset base. In other words, once we put up our money for this there are no additional fees or expenses at all on this whatsoever. There are no other associated costs -- no other expenses, nothing else. We're paying for drilling the wells and that's it. No expenses, no fees, no cushion and no need to have extra money sitting around for a cushion. The oil drilling company is responsible for any fees for drilling so there is no cushion or extra money needed for this.

No overhead. There are no office expenses, no salaries, no baloney, nobody's getting paid anything at all unless there's oil hit and then we benefit that way.

Fifth, we are not wildcatting. There is no wildcatting, which is a total advantage to you and I. They're drilling next to existing wells where there is proven oil production already, and we're using the geological reports to see exactly where the pockets of oil are at right now. That gives us a total advantage over any other drilling program where they're just speculating and guessing that oil might be in the area.

Last, and best of all, it's a turnkey program, so we don't have to be involved in any way, shape or form. We can just let the oil drilling company do their job and monitor what's happening. We will have someone on the ground there watching every single thing, day by day.

Here's how it works. Gross revenue comes in, net income from the drilling goes right to us as distributable cash. It goes from gross revenues and then right to our pockets from the refinery, from the accountants. That's the fast way to get paid. Take a look at the chart on the following page.

ROI	15 Wells	14 Wells	13 Wells	12 Wells	11 Wells	10 Wells	9 Wells	8 Wells	7 Wells	6 Wells	5 Wells	4 Wells	3 Wells	2 Wells	1 Well
95 BBLs	188.6	180.0	170.1	160.3	150.1	139.4	128.3	116.6	104.4	91.6	78.2	64.1	49.3	33.8	17.3
90 BBLs	178.7	170.1	161.2	151.9	142.2	132.1	121.5	110.5	98.9	86.8	74.0	60.8	46.7	32.0	16.4
85 BBLs	168.8	160.7	152.2	143.4	134.3	124.7	114.8	104.3	93.4	82.0	70.0	57.4	44.1	30.2	15.5
80 BBLs	158.8	151.2	143.3	135.0	126.4	117.4	108.0	98.2	87.9	77.1	65.9	54.0	41.5	28.0	14.6
75 BBLs	148.9	141.8	134.3	126.6	118.5	110.1	101.3	92.0	82.4	72.3	61.7	50.6	38.9	26.6	13.7
70 BBLs	139.0	132.3	125.4	118.1	110.6	102.7	94.5	85.9	76.9	67.5	57.6	47.3	36.3	24.9	12.8
65 BBLs	129.0	122.9	116.4	109.7	102.7	95.4	87.8	79.8	71.4	62.7	53.5	43.9	33.8	23.1	11.9
60 BBLs	119.1	113.4	107.4	101.3	94.8	88.0	81.0	73.6	65.9	57.9	49.4	41.0	31.2	21.3	10.9
55 BBLs	109.2	104.0	98.5	92.8	86.9	80.7	74.3	67.5	60.4	53.0	45.3	37.1	28.6	19.5	8.0
50 BBLs	99.3	94.5	89.5	84.4	79.0	73.4	67.5	61.4	54.9	48.2	41.2	33.8	26.0	17.8	9.1
45 BBLs	89.3	85.1	80.6	75.9	71.1	66.0	60.8	55.2	49.4	43.4	37.0	30.4	23.4	16.0	8.2
40 BBLs	79.4	75.6	71.6	67.5	63.2	58.7	54.0	49.1	44.0	38.6	32.9	27.0	20.8	14.2	7.3
35 BBLs	69.5	66.2	62.7	59.1	55.3	51.4	47.3	43.0	38.5	33.8	28.8	24.6	18.2	12.4	6.4
30 BBLs	59.6	56.7	53.7	50.6	47.4	44.0	40.5	36.8	33.0	28.9	24.7	20.3	15.6	10.7	5.5
25 BBLs	49.6	47.3	44.8	42.2	39.5	36.7	33.8	30.7	27.5	24.1	20.6	16.9	13.0	8.9	4.6
20 BBLs	39.7	37.8	35.8	33.8	31.6	29.3	27.0	24.5	22.0	19.3	16.5	13.5	10.4	7.1	3.6
15 BBLs	29.8	28.4	26.9	25.3	23.7	22.0	20.3	18.4	16.5	14.5	12.3	10.1	7.8	5.3	2.7
10 BBLs	19.9	18.9	17.9	16.9	15.8	14.7	13.5	12.3	11.0	9.6	8.2	6.8	5.2	3.6	1.8
5 BBLs	9.9	9.5	9.0	8.4	7.9	7.3	6.8	6.1	5.5	4.8	4.1	3.4	2.6	1.8	1.0
0 BBLs	0.0	0.0	0.0	0.0	0.0	0.0	0.0	0.0	0.0	0.0	0.0	0.0	0.0	0.0	0.0

NOTE:
1. Wells are referring to total number of oil producing wells.
2. BBLs are referring to total number of daily oil production per well in barrels.
3. ROI refers to yearly return of investment on a per unit basis. ROI for ½ and ¼ Units are the same. All ROI figures are shown in percentages and are based on a price point of $75 per barrel.

117

Look on the right side of the chart. Here's an example of what would happen if we only hit one well. At $90 a barrel, our return is approximately 16 percent on our money. That's kind of saying that if we only hit one well out of 15, we're still making 16 percent return, and that's every year until the well goes dry. That could be 10 or 15 years even. In my opinion, to get 16 percent on our money, if they only hit one well is what I feel is probably the worst case scenario because of the fact that they have the geological reports and they're drilling next to existing wells.

But let's say that we did go by our scenario of hitting our baseline. Now, the baseline is 10 wells. If you look at the top of the chart where it shows 10 wells, and follow that down to the highlighted box and look over to your left, it shows 65 barrels per day. If we use our conservative baseline that we told you earlier, the baseline is 65 barrels a day with 10 wells that struck oil out of 15.

Using these figures, our projected return is 95 percent if we hit 10 wells out of 15. Now, if we hit more than 10 wells, it goes up. If we get more barrels per day, like 90 barrels instead of 65, then our percentages go up. This chart is just a gauge of what could happen and where we could end up depending on how many wells we hit.

We can clearly see from this chart what would happen if we hit only seven wells instead of 15. Seven wells based on 65 barrels per day gives us 71 percent a year on our money. 71 percent return every year for as long as the well is pumping oil. We can take this chart and look around to see what the worst case scenario is all the way up to the best scenario and see what could happen. This is exciting, because as you can see, the potential here is quite good. And the fact that they happen to know where the oil is and have a pretty good idea they're going to hit it is strong. I think that you'll find that this investment is well worth taking a shot at.

We need to go ahead and look at some other things here. Remember that this is just an illustration and that obviously you have to look at all the private placement documents to get your comfort level. This has been just a general overview; the private placement documents will explain all the nuts and bolts and will have all the details you need to move forward.

Remember, this is a turnkey investment. And yes, there's risk involved. There's risk involved in everything that we do in our investing career, but we have to measure the risk and decide what is our downside and what is our potential upside; and allocate enough money to make it work, but not over-allocate.

For example, you never want to put too much money into something that has higher risk because of the potential of it not working. But again, the risk is extremely low in this particular program. If the risk is low, then we could easily allocate money that would make sense for your portfolio.

I would suggest definitely reading the this chapter again closely, and to think about your risk tolerance, depending on your age, your risk tolerance, your net worth, and on what type of goals you have to achieve.

If you're looking for growth, then this is the way to go, because this is probably the fastest way to get ahead, and probably the most calculated. This is a calculated investment with a calculated risk that probably will be well worth every penny we put into it.

I hope this answers your questions about what to look for when you invest in oil and gas drilling programs, but again this particular program is different than all the others that you've seen or that I've seen and that nothing else is like this. This is an incredible chance to be able to invest in drilling programs that are not like the others that you and I have seen.

Turnkey Investment Secret Strategy #5

FOREX

Turnkey Out of the Box Investment Secret Number 5 involves Forex trading. You may have heard of Forex trading or even tried it a bit yourself. In this chapter, I'm going discuss what Forex trading is, as well as the benefits and advantages and the risks involved. This is very valuable information, and I think you're going to find that there's a good reason why Forex trading is popular and quite successful, more so than stocks and mutual funds. So please take this information, and I hope that it will help you to get ahead.

First, let's address the question, what is foreign exchange trading? Foreign exchange trading is what we call "Forex" also sometimes annotated as FX. The Forex market is a worldwide financial market. It's huge. It's for the trading of world currencies. Don't let that intimidate you. This Turnkey Investment program will allow the average investor to invest in and profit from another exclusive market, foreign currency exchange, with very little money and no experience. I'll be more specific about this in the following pages.

Forex trading used to be different than the way we do it today. You used to have to have millions of dollars to invest in Forex. It was mostly institutional trading, but now it is opened up to pretty much everyone. People can invest in Forex just as if they were investing in the stock market. It's simplified, where even small investors can put in money and benefit from it. Now, pretty much everyone is able to go ahead and invest in Forex one way or another. But it is best to have your money managed for you by an experienced Forex trader.

How Forex Works

Forex trading is the simultaneous buying of one currency and selling of another. When you trade in the Forex market, you're buying or selling in currency pairs. If you sell the U.S. dollar to buy Japanese yen, that's a simple example of currency trading. You're leveraging the markets and trading against one for another. Profits can be realized by speculating on the price changes of each currency pair. So these prices will change daily, and you're able to benefit from those price changes.

The foreign exchange market is the most traded financial market in the world, doing over $4 trillion dollars each trading day. The market is open continually, 24 hours a day, starting at 10 am Monday in Sydney, Australia and stays open until 5:00 pm eastern time on Friday in New York. The trading markets open and close continuously as the trading day opens and closes across world time zones.

There is no centralized market place for Forex; currencies are traded on an over-the-counter basis in whichever market is open at that time. If you wanted to, you could trade currencies 24 hours a day, five days a week. With the exception of weekends, there is always a market open somewhere.

Currency values fluctuate throughout the day as various financial reports are announced across the globe. Everything from new home starts, unemployment rates, GNP, retail sales, seasonal crop production or even storms that stop production cold (think of the tsunami in Japan) affect the value of a country's currency. Forex traders attempt to capitalize on the fluctuations, basically betting that a currency will fluctuate up or down based on input of this type.

As I mentioned earlier, Forex is traded in pairs, basically one currency against another. For example, EUR/USD. When one currency is bought, the other is simultaneously sold. You are exchanging one country's currency for another's.

It is estimated that 75% - 80% of daily Forex trading volume is made up of the seven most frequently traded pairs which are referred to as "the majors." The US dollar is a partner in every one of the major pairs because it is the central currency against which all the other currencies are traded. There are, of course, other trading pairs that do not involve the USD but that do include the other major currencies. These pairs are referred to as cross-currency pairs.

Currency pair quotes are listed with the three letter country code, for example EUR/USD which is, obviously, the Euro and the US dollar. The first currency listed is called the Base Currency. In the above pair, the Euro is the Base Currency. The second currency listed is the Counter Currency. The Base Currency is always listed as "1". So a quote of EUR/USD 1.4251 means that the Euro is equal to 1.4251 US dollars. If the currency goes up, that means the Euro can now buy more US dollars.

Currency trades are always quoted in two prices. The "bid" which is the price you can sell the currency at and the "ask" which is the price you can buy the currency at. The difference between the two is the spread.

The currency fluctuations are measured in units called PIPS or Percentage in Points. The major currencies, are priced out to four decimal points, except for the Japanese Yen (which goes to two). So, for the most part, a PIP is $1/100^{th}$ of one percent. So if a currency pair is trading at an exchange rate of EUR/USD 1.4000 and the rate changes to 1.4010, then the price ratio increased 10 PIPS.

As you can see, the trades are made based on incredibly small, incremental movements of one currency against another. Because the Forex is traded over the counter as opposed to one centralized marketplace, there is the possibility of having not one single exchange rate but rather, a number of different exchange rates for each currency pair at any given time. In practice, the rates are very close.

Here's the thing: I know people who have "paper traded" the Forex for up to two years before they felt confident enough to start making trades. These are smart people, money people. Just about any Forex site you visit will offer a chance to paper (or practice) trade because they know it is very difficult to understand the process. Once they start trading, they are up at 3:30 in the morning to catch the London open and stay glued to their computer screens all day usually until the New York market closes.

This is not investing. Trading Forex is a job and a difficult one at that. It takes a lot of skill, experience and practice. And you have to be online constantly to catch the upticks and downticks when they happen. That's a lot of work and a lot of your time.

Trading Forex should be done by an expert. Instead of me trying to trade Forex and be an expert at it, I just give my funds to an expert and let them trade it and take a percentage of the profits. I do that with all my investments. Rather than try to be an expert in Forex or an expert in real estate, you're better off letting people who are experts in that field handle your money and get a piece of the action, because they're going to make fewer mistakes than you are. Why would you open yourself up to mistakes and have to go through all that learning curve and waste money?

Our program provides investors with an opportunity to have their money managed by some of the world's top Forex currency traders with solid track records. These traders have measurable risk results. It is so important that you are able to check results and we work with traders who have lengthy, measurable track records so you can go back and see how they've done in the best of times and the worst of times.

Why Invest in Forex?

There are some strong benefits in investing in the currency markets. Number one, as I mentioned before, the Forex market is probably the largest, most liquid market in the world. It's a $4 trillion dollar a day market. That's huge. So even though you may not have heard about it very much or at all, it is the largest market in the world. That's a lot of money flowing through. You want to have a piece of it.

The Forex is not linked to other investments. For example, it's not tied to the S&P 500. It's not tied to the stock market. It's not tied to bonds. It's not tied to mutual funds. It's pretty much set apart, separate from everything. As you know, stocks can be very unpredictable. It's a little bit more predictable with Forex, because you can track trades more easily.

It's also great for diversifying your portfolio, because many of you do have stocks or mutual funds, but you do not have any Forex. I would suggest you make sure you have some Forex in your portfolio but also make sure it is being managed by an expert. By that I don't mean buy and trade Forex on your own.

Now, the returns in Forex have been known to be quite high. Trading in Forex, your returns could potentially be ten, twenty, or even thirty percent. That's typical of what I have seen, and many of my colleagues who trade Forex or have Forex traded for them have better returns than most stocks and mutual funds. So Forex sometimes can beat most stock traders and most S&P 500 traders.

Risks

Protecting your downside, as I've mentioned often, is just as important as trying to figure out how much you can make. It's important to know how much you can lose in any investment. This is something investors must think about. How much risk can you take? If you can afford some risk, then it's very worthwhile to try this. If you cannot afford risk, then you shouldn't be doing anything speculative. Conversely, without risk, you can't get ahead.

Our partnership that we work with on Forex has a strong commitment to safety, and they feel that safety should take priority and precedence over the effort to achieve high returns. As with any investment, there are risks. With Forex, there are definitely ways to keep your risks significantly lower than when you're trying to trade other things, such as stocks.

You can lower your risk by using less money or by trading less frequently. You can also put stop-losses in place to protect against any potential downside. You can decide upfront how much risk you want to take.

In addition, you will find this is a very liquid market. You can get in and out in an instant. Anyone who has ever been stuck in an investment and unable to liquidate it knows how important this is.

Benefit from the Experts

It's important to have a money manager who pays attention to risk and cares about not losing money, someone who's not going to be a cowboy and just guess. It needs someone who has a strategy in place and a turnkey system for you that you can just put money in and have it traded for you on your behalf and benefit from the results. Our partners are ranked number one and consist of award-winning investment managers with over 20 years' experience. They definitely have a provable track record to show you their results, not only on the good trades, but the ones that didn't work out so well.

They still are excellent, excellent, excellent in their field and are able to get good returns, even when they don't win every trade. That's important because no Forex trader wins at every trade. No investor in any type of investment wins at every trade. Smart investors know that they will lose at some point and they take measures to ensure that their losses are minimized. One of the reasons why I chose to work with the people we do is that their risk adjustment is excellent. In other words, they measure the risk and the downside and invest accordingly. So when you get a chance to look at the track record, I'm sure you'll find that it's been phenomenal, and the risk is measurable. The partners are people who are founders of public and private firms with over 20 years of experience, and they're used to managing risk. They are financial consultants and are experts in what they do.

With over 20 years of trading and portfolio management experience, our money managers know the ins and outs of this market. They've been trading and managing portfolios for two decades, and their track record is one of the least volatile, lowest risk and highest return track records that I have seen in the money management industry. You definitely need to take a close look at it, and you want to ask the right questions.

You want to be sure to ask, "Show me your track record. Show me your losses. Show me your gains. What have you averaged? And how have you done during the worst times, let alone the best times?"

So those are the things to look for when investing money into foreign currencies with a Forex trader. What is the benefit to you as an investor when you're investing into a Forex trading program? Well, you have world class risk control using strict parameters to protect investors' money. They have their systems in place and tools in place to protect from downside, to protect from losing more than you want to lose.

How the Program Works

The trading account is opened in your name and it will be traded for you at a reputable brokerage firm or bank. You have complete access to your account at any time. You can see any trades going on at any time. Twenty-four hours a day, you have access to your accounts.

One of the reasons why we invest in Forex is because it is a diversified way to protect from losses in the stock market or mutual funds. For those of you who are not certain where the stock market will go, by investing in Forex, you are spreading out your risk and diversifying into other investments that would then protect you from stock market crashes. Forex is totally unrelated to stock market. It has no correlation whatsoever.

Proprietary Systems

Our experts' proprietary multi-strategy systems focus on high probability, low-risk trades. In other words, their matrix is set up to get the highest potential gains with the downside risks significantly lower than the potential gain. Forex trading can be extremely profitable, especially if they have stop-losses in place to protect on the downside and then make more on the upside. So the idea, as with everything, is to win more than you lose.

Whether you are trading in the stock market or in Forex, you're placing bets on trading. You're betting that you're going to have more wins than losses, and only a good money manager who has systems in place can do this for you. Doing it on your own is not easy and I would not recommend it at all. You're better off going with a turnkey system, where you put your money to work and you benefit from the results of a proven track record.

Remember, when you're trading in Forex, and you invest in a program like the ones that we do, you can take your money out any time that you want. At the end of the day, if you decide that you don't want to do it anymore, that's it. You can withdraw the funds at any time. And of course, there's no penalty to take the money out.

Use Your IRA

You can even use your IRA to trade Forex. We can help you set up your IRAs and old 401(k) plans so that you're able to use this for Forex, and of course, other investments, as well. While there are no penalties to withdraw the money out of the Forex trading program, there would be 0penalties to withdraw funds from your IRA. You don't want to take it out of your IRA, but it's okay to stop trading or stop investing in anything that you're ever doing.

Investment and Fees

The minimum investment for Forex trading for the program that we've been using is $10,000, and that means that they'll invest your $10,000 with low risk and get the maximum return they possibly can. Again, I've seen anywhere from between 10 and 20 percent returns a year or more, depending on the trader's track record. I've gathered up the best traders that I could find that have proven to me that they won't lose all my money, and they will probably make money for me, more so than most. Returns on investment can vary, but I have seen returns that definitely exceed most stock market transactions. The good thing is that you have the ability to potentially make more money than if you were investing in stocks and mutual funds.

When your account is traded, if you make profits, the traders/partners then take 30 percent of the profit. They're doing all the work. They're doing everything they can to make money for you, and their performance fee is 30 percent of the profit. That's typically what most traders would get for trading my money.

For example, if I invested $10,000 and my trader were to make 60 percent on my money that would be $6,000. They would end up taking 30 percent of that, which I feel is good, because they're doing the work and I can free up all my time to do something else.

I let them trade it and do a good job and they probably do a much better job than I can on my own. More importantly, I don't want to sit in front of a computer screen all day long trading foreign currencies.

They have an administration fee of 2% annually, which is of the amount that's being managed. So every year, your fee is 2% of the total amount that is being managed in your portfolio. If they do well, they make money. If they don't make money, they don't get any performance fee. They do not make 30 percent of your money if they didn't make anything for you. But since they do, and since they have a good track record, the chances of them making money and you making money are very good. So that's very exciting to me.

Now remember, the performance fees are based solely on profit. So there's no performance fee charged at all unless the account achieves new net high profits after accounting for prior fees. In other words, after the fees are removed from the previous transactions, if there are profits going forward, then, they'll get paid. If not, then they don't make any money unless you make money. I like that. It's a built-in incentive for them to make money.

This policy results in the fairest treatment for the client, and it's for your benefit. Now, let's say for example, that you are a larger client, and you would like to have a customized portfolio. What that means is that if you're a higher net worth investor or an institutional client with substantial assets, they will tailor a specific portfolio for you that may be lower risk or higher risk depending on your risk tolerance.

Let's say that you want to take more risk, and you want to do more than what the normal trading program will be. They would go ahead and do so based on your discretion and your desires. Or let's say that you want less risk. There are ways to reduce the risk, and it's very simple. Less risk equals less return. So they can easily lower the risk by lowering the return and vice versa.

They will certainly analyze your portfolio to see what it is that you want to do. So of course, they'll sit with you and go over your current situation to determine what your risk tolerance is and what you would like to achieve and how you want to achieve that. They will spend the time with you to figure out what's going to be best for you. So if you are a higher net worth client, and you're looking to have something customized for you, then you should sit with them and learn exactly what it is that they can do for you and measure the risks.

Turnkey Investment Secret Strategy #6

AUCTION HOUSES

Turnkey Out of the Box Investment Secret Number Six is the system I use to invest in foreclosed, bank-owned houses. This is a program that is done-for-you and I'm sure probably different from what you've heard before. I am about to show you how to acquire bank auction properties through a partnership and get them rehabbed for you.

It's critical to know the things to look for when trying to find the right partner who can fix and flip properties for you. I'm going to give you the criteria and show you the things that I look for when I partner with someone to have them fix and flip houses right from the bank auctions.

The particular area that I'm going to teach you about is in Las Vegas. The reason Las Vegas is my prime focus right now is because of the fact that Las Vegas was hit the hardest by this current economic downturn: It has the worst decline in property values and probably the highest foreclosure rate in the United States. I'm sure there are other bad areas but this one is definitely one of the most devastated.

Why do we buy real estate in areas that have taken the worst hits? Well, it's kind of obvious. We're going to be able to get the best prices!

I'm going to show you our system: Exactly how our partners find houses at auction and then fix them and flip them for us without our having to do anything.

We're Florida-based and we've done quite a few deals here in Florida, but unlike Florida, this program gives investors access to bank houses that are purchased by local experts right at the auction. You can see exactly how we buy them from the auction and you'll be able to see exactly what our process is. When you come with us to visit, you will see how the entire process works, from pre-auction to final re-sale.

All real estate is local. Our partners in this strategy are on the ground in Las Vegas and they are local experts. They've been doing this quite a long time. They will bid on, repair and sell the foreclosed homes on your behalf in the hardest hit market in the United States. The advantage is that the spreads are very good and they are able to buy, fix and flip properties quite quickly, typically in 90 to 120 days.

How do you benefit from this type of program? If you partner with us and invest in our Turnkey Foreclosure Auction House program, you could end up making approximately 30 to 40 percent per year on your investment. That's a typical average and that is based on the current situation. If the market changes later on down the road then we would either be in a better off situation or lesser situation, depending on the market change. Currently, we are making between 30 to 40 percent profit per year on our money.

I want you to realize that this can be done because there's a turnkey system in place. How do you make profits without having to go out and do it yourself? Doing it yourself is obviously a pain in the neck and difficult. Almost all the programs I've seen teach you how to do it yourself. They teach you how to find the property, fix the property and get the property sold.

Well, I can tell you that if you're doing it on your own, the process is excruciatingly difficult if not impossible in many cases. It's always better to let a turnkey system that has a staff of people, a system and a coordinated team do it for you. That's why I believe in turnkey, done-for-you systems like this one.

Once you have shown proof of funds and let us know that you want to be involved, we want to be totally transparent and show you our entire turnkey system. We will fly you out and put you up for two free nights in Las Vegas so you can see everything from beginning to end. It's important for you to see Las Vegas from a real estate perspective – the areas that are growing, the areas that have stopped growing and are declining and to realize that Las Vegas is not only a viable market, but a fantastic opportunity. We want you to see first-hand the types of properties you will be investing in and how our system works.

Here's how the process works: You'd fly to Las Vegas typically on a Sunday morning. Our partners pay for your airfare and your hotel. You'll stay at a hotel such as the beautiful Mandalay Bay or The Trump Hotel. That's the caliber of hotels that we use.

Once there, you'll go on the foreclosure tour. We'll take you on a tour of the different subdivisions that have brand new homes that are only a few years old that need very little repair. The tour of the actual houses will give you an opportunity to see properties in each phase: The before, during and after. You'll see what the condos and houses look like, what types of repairs need to be done and how easy it is. Remember, because this is a turnkey system, our partners in Las Vegas handle the repairs and no money comes out of your pocket for paying for repairs or any expenses whatsoever. You're responsible for the purchase price and they're responsible for doing all the work.

Next, you go to the live auctions with our partners. They will show you how the auction works and exactly how they bid on these properties. Let's say, for example, there are 100 people at the auction. One of our buyers will be there all day from 10:00 in the morning on, bidding on these properties. You'll see for yourself that we're buying houses at unbelievable prices. Brand new, three bedroom, two bathroom houses for $90,000 that are worth $135,000 or $140,000 as is. That's exciting to me. The same thing goes with condos. We're buying condos for $40,000 that are currently worth $55,000 to $60,000. That's exciting.

You will visit the offices where our partners are, see how the entire operation works, including making sure the title is clear and closing procedures. You'll see how the real estate staff gets the properties moved in 90 to 120 days. They will also show you the HUD statements. You are going to see the actual numbers, the buys and the sells on a HUD statement, when they were bought, when they were sold, how much money was made.

Seeing the HUD statements and our operation will give you the proof that you would need to make the decision to get involved. We want the process to be transparent because we know that by seeing this firsthand, it will become very clear to you as to why this strategy is a pretty safe bet. The downside is very, very limited and the profit potential is good. They will show you their track record. They will take the time to show you how many houses were bought and sold in the last couple of years, exactly how long they were on the market and the profit for each one.

Downside Risk

Now, remember this, many people who are afraid to invest in real estate are worried about the market. They always say, "Well, what about the market? What if the market is still going to go down further?" Well, here's something to think about. When you're buying a house and flipping it in 120 days, then even if the price fluctuated up or down a couple of thousand dollars, it does not make a difference in the whole scheme of things.

For example, maybe today we buy a house at $90,000 and sell it for $130,000. But then let's say next week we buy a house for $89,000 and sell it for $129,000. No problem. The market doesn't move fast enough to make a difference in that short of timeframe. When we're buying houses and flipping them in 120 days, the market's not going to change up or down enough to make a difference. If you're buying and holding, that's a different story. Of course there's downside risk if you're going to just sit on it and hold it, but again, we are dealing in short-term flips that are not nearly as affected by market fluctuations.

I'm not worried about the prices in Las Vegas. Whether the prices are at the bottom or not, I can buy a property at whatever price it's at right now today, turn around and sell it within 120 days and still make the profit I need. I don't care if the houses are cheaper next time I buy. All that means is that the next time I go to buy, instead of paying $90,000, I may pay $85,000. That works for me. If I pay $85,000 and sell it at $125,000, the spread is the same.

The point is that I'm not worried about the market. I'm worried about *NOT* being in the market. Because to me, not investing in bank-owned houses is foolish. You have to position yourself to take advantage of this. One of the biggest things that has hit our economy is all of these homes that are in foreclosure. And anytime something bad has happened in the economy, there has always been a solution and a way that people will benefit from it.

My feeling is that we want to be very greedy when times are bad and people are fearful. When times are good and the market is good and at the top, we do not want to invest. We want to be a seller. We want to be out of our properties completely and we do not want to be involved.

Right now with these particular prices so low and the strong potential upside, we want to stay involved and we want accumulate as many properties and flip them as fast as we can to get the results we'd like. So it does not matter what the price of the house is now or what the market is doing because they get bought and sold in such a short time frame that it does not affect your risk factor here.

Again, here's an example of what happens. November's price to sell a property might have been $150,000. December's price might have been $149,000 and January's price might have been $148,000. As you can see, these differences are not significant enough for us to have to worry about. We're not going to hold these for two, three or four years. We're talking about 120 days to flip these houses and therefore, the market makes no difference in this case.

Doing Foreclosure Deals: The Right Way and the Wrong Way(s)

Now there are three different ways to do a foreclosure deal. This is one of our secrets that I want to share with you. There are two wrong ways and one right way. Let's start with the wrong ways.

First of all, trying to negotiate a foreclosure with a homeowner is too much work. It's unnecessary and not worth your time. It's very difficult to find an owner who wants to talk to you personally. They always want to shut the door and do not want to talk to people coming to their door bothering them. That's the first mistake that people make. They try to go knock on a door and say, "Hey, look, I see you're in trouble, let's go ahead make a deal." That's not the way to do it.

If you're trying to get a property from an individual owner, there's more aggravation and there's not as much money to be made as you could buying it from an auction. The person who's in foreclosure and losing their house is dealing in terms of their purchase price; they want or need to get X amount of money.

Owners refuse to or simply can't take a hit or a discount on their property. They do not want to reduce the price. They want to keep it where it is. Typically, in today's market, the house is upside down and therefore there's no equity available. Simply put, trying to negotiate with an individual is really too much work, not necessary and true deals are few and far between. That's why that system is difficult and hardly anybody makes money doing it.

In this Turnkey Investment Strategy, we are getting the properties after the bank has taken back the property. By the time a property reaches the auction, the bank is selling it at huge discounts -- *huge discounts*. The bank that takes a property back is going to sell that property for much less than you'd get it for if you were talking to a private owner. You don't want to talk to a homeowner. Why not go to the auction and bid on it and get it cheaper than anybody else and take advantage of the bank's losses?

The second wrong way is trying to get a short sale at the bank or buy an REO. The bank controls the deal. It refuses to accept your offer and now you're negotiating back and forth, which slows down the process. If you're personally calling the bank or even walking in to submit offers, you're going to have some definite challenges. The main problem is that there are multiple offers coming in for the same property at the bank and you don't know what those offers are. You're not at an auction; you cannot hear what the bids are. You put in a silent bid and if your bid is high enough, you get it. If you're not, you lose it. It's very hit or miss and you have no control over the situation.

It typically takes the bank quite some time to accept your offer. When we do buy at the foreclosure auction, we are getting a bid in right there, real time and then as soon as the bid is won, we know immediately that we have a house. We don't have to wait two weeks, three weeks, four weeks to hear back from the bank to find out if they accepted our offer or not. That's a very big plus. Dealing directly with a bank to find bank-owned properties is a challenge. More importantly it's time-consuming and not an efficient use of your efforts.

Another reason that it's difficult to get good deals from a bank is because the houses are priced at current retail market value. A bank will try to price its properties in the same range that all the other bank-owned properties are selling for. Therefore, you're not getting a very good margin at all.

Banks will be difficult in that they may refuse to accept your offer when they have other bidders. But once it goes to the auction that means that they don't have the ability to sell it on their own and they're going to go ahead try to get rid of it at any price they possibly can to get it moved.

In other words, if in fact you had to do all this yourself and take the time out to do it, it's unproductive. It's difficult; it's a pain in the neck. You're always better off partnering with someone who already has a turnkey operation in place with direct connections with the bank or direct connections at the auction. They have the ability to make this stuff happen faster than you could on your own.

So here's the right way. The right way is the fastest way and the most productive way, which is foreclosure auction flips. These are the best deals because at an auction, the bank is trying to dump its property, dump its note and get rid of the property at a fire sale price. They just want it off the books at that point. They have not had any luck selling the property any other way and they want out. They want it *GONE*. That's the best time to take advantage and make the most of your money by buying properties at the right price.

In real estate, we make our money on the buy. When we buy at auction, we make our money going in because we buy the property so cheaply. If we are buying a house at $90,000 that's worth, as is, $110,000 on the MLS without even fixing it, then it's worth it to go ahead and buy a house for $90,000 and then clean it up, make it look brand new again and sell it for $130,000. That's an efficient way to make the money.

When you're bidding at an auction the biggest discounts are right before the note is auctioned off. When the bank is ready to put a property up at auction, that's when they have marked it down to the very least amount that they will take. That gives you a chance to go ahead and get the best possible price. I think it's an awesome plan. I love the way that works.

Partnering with Turnkey Experts

What are the advantages to partnering with a group that has a turnkey investment system? If you're investing in a turnkey foreclosure auction property group that's going to find, fix and flip properties for you, everything is done for you. That means you don't have to get any bids, you don't have to mess with any repairs, you don't have to find the property, you don't have to fix it and you don't have to sell it. All of that is done for you.

Yes, you could do it yourself but it would be difficult. It would take more time. And what is your time worth? Using a turnkey system is valuable because it frees up all of your time. What can you do with your time if it's done for you? What could you be doing with your time if you invested your money with a group that does it for you and you put your time into something else?

Investing is having your money work for you. If you are swinging a hammer or negotiating deals, you are working a job, not investing. There are many other things you can do with your time while your money is working for you. Let me show you how it works. We will show you everything from beginning to end: How to bid at the auction, how to fix and flip a house and how you can then partner with us and have us do it for you.

The Nuts and Bolts

You are in control of what you buy. If you tell us, "Well, I can only afford a condo for $40,000" then that's where we'll start.

If you said, "I can afford up to $100,000" then that's where we'll start. You are in control of how much money you spend for this particular flipping program.

Also, the property goes in your name. This is very important. The property is not in the partner's name, the property is in your name. What happens is they end up sharing the revenues with you. When they sell the house, after paying the expenses, the realtor fees and closing costs, the profit is phenomenal. There's plenty of money to share so by having a good chunk of net profit, you make out like a bandit and had not one bit of effort. No worries, no aggravation, nothing to do. That's pretty exciting.

The partnership in Las Vegas will have their team of people look at all the houses that are available the morning prior to bidding on the property. Before they ever go bid on the property, their staff physically looks at all of the properties. The auction opens up Monday morning at 10:00 a.m. So before 10:00 a.m., their team of seven people goes out and looks at 200 homes. That's how many homes are coming on the market every day.

Two hundred homes a day are being auctioned off at the auction. Not all of those are good deals. Out of 200 homes, maybe 50 of them are really good, sweet deals. That means the properties are in good condition; they may only need $3,000 worth of repairs or $5,000 worth of repairs or $7,000. Or maybe there's no tenant in them. If there's a tenant in them, then we know that it's going to cost of a couple thousand dollars to pay to have them move out. We pay a tenant $2,000 or less to give us their keys and move out of the house right then and there. That, of course, is factored into our costs, but a house without a tenant is better than a house with a tenant.

Just a note: The partnership will get the tenant out for you. They will go to the tenant and kindly offer them some money to give the keys over and to move out of the house so we can repair the property and get it off the books. In other words, there's no reason why you have to go deal with any tenants; they do it all for you. There's no worries, no fears. That's another advantage to being part of this turnkey system. Everything is done with a system by experienced, professional people. A well-oiled machine.

At 4:00 in the morning, six or seven guys go out into the field and inspect these houses. Number one, the properties are all in the same subdivision, so that makes the process more efficient. They know the streets. They can whip in and out of the streets and look at these houses and look in the windows and see if there's damage. They can look at the outside and in many cases they can get inside the houses. There's either a lock box on the door and they have the code or some of the houses were left open. They can go in and look at the property, evaluate it and then get a report to the bidder before 10:00 a.m.

All of the data that was collected in the morning goes to the bidder and the bidder now knows that there are 50 houses out of 200 that he will bid on. He also knows that your money is sitting there and my money's sitting there and it's ready to go to buy a house at the auction for cash and close on it and have it flipped in 120 days.

WHY LAS VEGAS WORKS FOR US

Increase in Hotels Rooms = Increase in Jobs

On the next page you'll see a chart of the metropolitan area hotel rooms. As you can see, the number of rooms in thousands is on the left-hand side. It shows 40 up to 160. What this is saying is that the number of people who are moving to Las Vegas is increasing, even to this day, because of the hotel rooms going in.

The Encore and The Wynn Hotels are fairly new. Those have been built there just recently. Those are excellent hotels right near where we're buying these houses. This area has four or five different hotels that you're going to see when you travel there with us. You'll see exactly what the growth is. There are a lot of new things going up. There's new construction going on to finish another major project.

Time Magazine did an entire cover article talking about how good Las Vegas is. They're still saying that Las Vegas is one of the hottest places to be. Why? Jobs, for starters. Every time a hotel or casino goes up, each room in the hotel creates three more jobs. People will move from other states to come and work in Las Vegas and those people will need housing. More hotel rooms equals more jobs, more people moving. There are definitely still thousands of people moving into Las Vegas every day because of all the jobs that are there, whether its casinos or whether it's internet or whatever it may be. In fact, many of them have jobs just in computers where they do not leave their home. But Las Vegas has a growing job market that attracts people.

A second point is that Las Vegas is an inexpensive place to live because the homes are cheap. People will continue to move there because it's affordable. Why wouldn't you want to buy a house, a brand new house for $100,000 that was $250,000? Affordability is as much an attraction factor as the job market.

Despite the economy, the county still sees a huge growth. There are still tons of people moving there and that tells me that there's still going to be a continuous demand to get these houses sold quickly. And yes, they do get sold quickly. They are selling under market on the MLS by a strong sales team. And the houses are sold sometimes for cash, sometimes for part financing. As long as we hold the houses for 60 days, there are no seasoning issues.

Increase in Visitors

Visitors are still growing consistently as well. There are thousands and thousands of visitors every year, and the rate of visitors is still continuously growing. This chart goes through 2011, and as you can see, the growth is still there. Las Vegas had a little bit of a dip there in 2009, like everything else did, but picked back up again and here we are now with more visitors just like nothing ever happened. So,

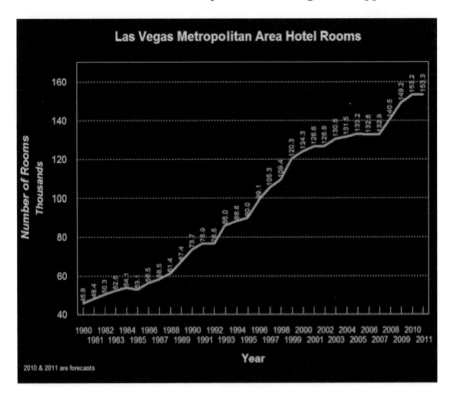

even the tougher economy is still not stopping people from visiting. Millions of people are visiting Las Vegas for conventions and everything else. And that creates a big need for housing.

Airport Expansion

The McCarran Airport is going through its second year of a five year and $4 billion renovation expansion. Nearly 50 percent of all visitors to southern Nevada go through McCarran Airport. The airport is going to be expanded by 50 percent. Every new hotel room built means 320 new passengers annually at the airport. So every time there's a new hotel room built, 320 people annually come through this airport just for that. This has been true for the last 20 years. There are over 30,000 new hotel rooms scheduled to be completed in the next four to five years -- 30,000! That means that the airport will expect an additional 10 million passengers by the end of 2015.

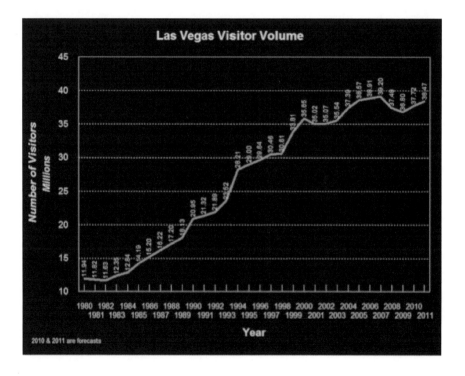

Convention Center Expansion

Las Vegas is the number one hot spot for conventions in the world and in order to maintain that position, Las Vegas is putting money into expanding its Convention Center – around $900 million dollars. Millions of people go to Las Vegas for seminars, conventions, etc. Not just to Las Vegas, but to the actual Convention Center. It's the world's largest meeting place – the number one convention destination in the world.

The Opportunity

As I mentioned earlier, we make our money, you and I, when we invest in a property and we buy it at a big discount. We buy it right. We bid on a house and we buy it for dirt cheap. Repairing the house doesn't affect the overall net profit that much. The net profit is there because we're buying it at such a big discount.

The houses in Vegas are what I consider a steal. Well, foreclosures are up 300 percent. So are there plenty of foreclosures? Tons of foreclosures. The prices have dropped to levels not seen for a decade. I mean really, what a difference. The prices today are where they were ten years ago.

So let me recap how flipping auction houses works. First of all, we're buying properties at unbelievable prices -- around 55 cents on the dollar. That's about 30 cents on the high market price of 2007. We flip them retail for a huge return, usually around $11,000 net profit on a $100,000 house.

Each property has about an $11,000 net profit to you on a $100,000 house. You as the investor would take home around $10,000 or $11,000 per house, per flip. Now, if you take that and do that four or five times a year, that will add up. What if your investment money was turned four times for the year? You made $10,000 four times. That's $40,000 on a $100,000 house. That's 40 percent because your investment was turned four times. On some occasions, we've been able to turn the investment five times in a year. Either way, whether it's flipped three times, four times or five times for the year, that return is just phenomenal. It's unbeatable. It's hard to get that kind of return. And the risk is significantly low because we're buying the houses at such a huge discount.

We're looking at about 90 days by the time everything is done and then we repeat the process again, again and again using the same money. Your $100,000 will get a property bought, fixed and sold. Then we do it again. Bought, fixed and sold. Bought, fixed and sold. This will allow you to have your money working for you three or four times a year. This creates a big compounding affect. If you made $10,000 three times or four times for the year, imagine now you have enough money to buy another condo at the end of one year. By the end of two years, you're buying one new house for free. By the end of three years you're buying two or three more houses for free because you accumulated the compounding money from your efforts. It happens fast.

Now imagine you're doing all of this tax-free in a Roth IRA. Using your Roth IRA to do these trades, flipping properties, is what will get you the best advantage. So use your Roth IRA and do these transactions tax-free. Because you don't pay taxes on the profits, you can reinvest the entire amount again and again and again and grow your wealth ten times faster than doing the same deal outside of the Roth IRA.

This is critical to your success. Think about how you can do this using a tax-free Roth IRA.

And of course, if you were able to refer people to us for this program, we would compensate you for it. So if you refer friends to this turnkey system, I'll make sure you get rewarded for it.

Let me recap what happens when you come to visit my partners out there in Las Vegas, exactly how the procedure works.

Number one, you take a trip to Las Vegas and you come to a welcome dinner with everybody. Depending on when you come, that may be a Sunday night. You'll have a nice dinner with everybody together, getting to know everybody on a personal level.

Day number two you're going to look at houses and attend the auction. Our partners are going to spend time with you showing you how the bidding process works from beginning to end. You'll see the office set up, how the sales of the properties are handled and meet some members of our team.

On the third day, you can go ahead and enjoy Las Vegas on your own and do whatever you want to do. People come to Las Vegas to have fun and we want to make sure you get your share of it and you get a feel for the energy and buzz of what is really happening in Vegas.

It's important that you get a chance to see everything from beginning to end and we will, in fact, show you how the process works step-by-step. By the time you finish, you will have a complete understanding of the whole process. At the same time you'll have had your trip paid for, including airfare and a hotel right on the strip at either the MGM Grand or the Trump hotel or any of the other many good hotels along there.

Now, once your money is in our escrow account, our partners make an offer on a property and win a bid. Once they win a bid they inform you that, yes, you now own a house and it's in your name. The next step is to clean and repair the house and get it ready to put on the market. Then they will put the house on the market and sell it. It usually takes about 60 days to get a house rehabbed, marketed and sold. It takes on average about 30 days to go through all the closing transactions and make sure everything is done and out the door.

And then of course, we repeat the process, usually within two to three months. There are a lot of people who are involved in this process to make it work. And you're going to meet all these people. You're going to meet the researchers, the inspectors, the bidders

BUILD WEALTH TAX FREE

and the people that clean and repair the houses and all the agents who sell the houses on the backend. So come out and meet the team. It takes a big team of people to do this type of transaction. It's not possible to do it efficiently and effectively by yourself. It's difficult and it's too slow. Too many things get in the way.

Crunching the Numbers

The cash on cash return is phenomenal. These deals are done at the foreclosure auction and you're looking to make about 10 percent cash on cash return four times a year. Ten percent four times throughout the year works out to about 40 percent for the whole year. If it's done five times, let's say they're able to complete this transaction five times over the course of the year, then you're looking at 50 percent return on your money. That would be the best case scenario and I think that's a very possible thing. It's happened already.

Let's look at the numbers. You're able to preview and choose the type of house that you want, meaning that you can pick this subdivision or that subdivision. You can pick a house for $90,000 or $100,000. You can pick a condo for $40,000 or $50,000. You have some say in what you're going to buy. Once you've decided, then they do all the work.

You can put a limit on what they spend. You can say, "Look, I don't want to spend any more than $95,000." Then that's the cap. It gets put in place and that's the top amount that they will spend when they make a purchase for you.

The team bids on a house that meets your criteria, they clean it and list the house and get it sold with a Realtor® as soon as possible. Typically, cleaning and repairing a house is around $4,500. And remember that those costs are paid from the resale; you're not paying for it upfront. Those expenses come out at closing when the property is sold. So let's say the resale price was $140,000. A real estate commission for selling the house is $8,400, which pays for all the real estate transactions done. The profit is $22,000. And there is $22,000 is left over for profit, average per house. Twenty-two percent is a high cash on cash return on this flip. That is split with our partners 60/40.

Case Studies

On the next page, there's a map of where we are investing. There's Las Vegas downtown, where it says "A" right there. All around the area, there are subdivisions everywhere and you can see that there are major highways going in and going out of the city. All around there are pockets of brand new homes that I've looked at and inspected myself that I feel are excellent, excellent purchases.

Here are some examples for you to look at. You will see there are some differences as far as the square footage, how much the houses were bought for, what the current market is, but I want you to get an idea of what they look like.

391 Hidden Hole Drive, Las Vegas
Property Summary
Size: 1819 square feet
Number of bedrooms: 3
Number of bathrooms: 3
Size of garage: 2-car garage
Year built: 2005
Community: Rhodes Ranch
Status: Sold
Condition: Good

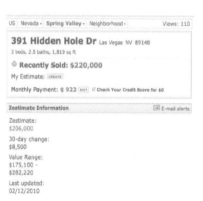

US : Nevada · Spring Valley · Neighborhood ·   Views: 110

391 Hidden Hole Dr Las Vegas NV 89148
3 beds, 2.5 baths, 1,819 sq ft

⬦ **Recently Sold:** $220,000

My Estimate: [CREATE]

Monthly Payment: $ 922 [RENT] ✓ Check Your Credit Score for $0

Zestimate Information   ✉ E-mail alerts

Zestimate:
$206,000

30-day change:
$8,500

Value Range:
$175,100 -
$282,220

Last updated:
02/12/2010

Financial Summary
Date purchased: 6/01/08
Amount paid at auction: $175,001
Square foot price paid: $ 96
Previous loan on house: $229,000
Current market value: $206,000

Profit
Bought at auction for: $175,001
Listed for resale for: $229,900
Sales contract price: $220,000
Gross profit: $44,999
Commissions and cost to fix up and fees: $17
Net profit: $27,548

72 day flip
14% cash on cash return
71% annual rate of return

Take a look at the Property Summary on the next page. That's exactly what you and I will be buying. Exactly. It's a phenomenal property; three bedroom, two bathrooms with a two-car garage. It was built in 2005, recently sold for $230,000. Unbelievable. The price paid at the auction was $175,000. That's phenomenal. It's hard to find those kinds of returns. When you look at this, here's one with the gross profit of $44,000. Not a bad deal. This was flipped in 72 days. This particular house was flipped in 72 days and brought a phenomenal return, done for you quick.

Here's another example. This house is 1,700 square feet, three bedroom, two and a half bathrooms, two-car garage, built in 2005. This is another perfect example of how easy it is to buy these brand new houses and then fix and flip them. This house was bought and sold in 44 days. And the return was 33 percent. Not a bad day.

Our job is to buy as many houses as we can for you on your behalf. We split the profits 60/40. Sixty percent goes to the group who does all the work; forty percent goes to you as an investor. I mentioned earlier that you also get paid for referring people. We pay a $1,000 bird dog fee, so if you find an investor for us, you get paid $1,000 per flip. And that's pretty easy because we fly them out there for free and no one says no. It's an obvious deal. They're very easy to do. If you're already investing with us, we pay $2,000 for each flip.

Property Summary
Size: 1,739 square feet
Number of bedrooms: 3
Number of bathrooms: 2.5
Size of garage: 2-car garage
Year built: 2005
Builder: Beazer
Community: Grand Teton Village
Status: vacant
Condition: very clean

Financial Summary
Date purchased: 8/24/09
Amount paid at auction: $81,000
Square foot price paid: $46.58
Previous loan on house: $330,000
Current market value: $127,000

Profit
Bought at auction for: $81,000
Listed for resale for: $129,900
Sales contract price: $132,000
Gross profit: $51,000
Commissions and cost to fix up and fees: $19,905
Net profit: $31,095

44 day flip
33.7 cash on cash return
276% annual rate of return

153

Remember, in anything there's always risk. We don't know what the real estate market will do but I tell you this, if it stays like it is, we'll be making a lot of money for the next five to 10 years with the same exact results. I hope that gives you a good example of how our turnkey system works and what process you want to do to go through all that.

BONUS INVESTMENT STRATEGY!

Private Money

Here at the Poggi Wealth Institute, one of the most common issues that our clients come to us about is the $5,000 per year contribution limit on IRAs. There are many ways to create strong returns in your IRA, but if you are limited as to how much you can contribute, how can you build your IRA quickly? Or what if you would like to invest more money with your IRA than you currently have? The information in this chapter is going to be critical to helping you grow your IRA above and beyond just the $5,000 per year contribution that you're going to make. I am going to share some of the secrets and strategies that I've learned over the years that I personally have used to help grow my IRA tax-free using private funding. Whether you are trying to make up for lost time or are looking for exponential growth in your IRA, this information is going to be extremely valuable for you.

If you don't have enough funds or you've already allocated all the funds in your IRA to investments, your next step is to find other funds outside of your IRA. I'm going to show you how to use other people's money to grow your wealth, make everyone happy and make everyone win.

Having access to private funds enables you to jump on deals as they come up and, of course, to do more deals. Using private lenders gives you an edge over your competition because they aren't leveraging other funds to grow their portfolios as fast as you can. In short, you can do more deals faster and leave your competition in the dust.

Who are these private lenders? When I say "private lenders," that could be a person, an individual, a company, a friend, a brother or sister. A private lender could be any individual who has some money to loan. It could be a neighbor. It could be someone that you met years ago. It could be someone you've dated or are dating or a spouse, anybody who could loan funds to you.

Private Money vs. Hard Money

Just to make sure we are on the same page here, I'm not talking about hard money lenders. A hard money lender charges points, and they have a very high interest rate. I'm talking about private lenders. There are millions of dollars sitting in IRAs that are not getting good returns and that could potentially be lent to you if you prove that you can do something with it and return the money.

A lot of times, private lenders do not charge points. Most are just looking for what they consider to be a "good" interest rate. Private money is where you're going to borrow from someone else's IRA, they're not going to charge you points, and you're not going to get creamed with upfront fees which increase the risk factor right from the very beginning, before you even make the transaction.

Private lenders are just ordinary people who are willing to loan money and would like a nice interest rate return. Let me give you another example. Let's say someone has an IRA, and right now, they have it in CDs or something of that sort, or they have an IRA and it's in mutual funds, and it's not earning money. If you offered that person a 6 percent guaranteed return or a 10 percent guaranteed return, give or take, if it's a solid deal, and they feel like they could put their money into it and be at less risk than mutual funds, which is just about everything, then it's a good bet that they will take a chance on you. You should definitely pursue that route.

It's easy to get private lenders to loan you funds if you present the opportunity in the proper way. No one's just going to invest with you if you say to someone, "Hey, look. I'd like to borrow some money. I have this great idea." You need to have a presentation prepared that would make them want to loan you the funds. They need to be convinced that it's a safe deal and a safe bet.

There's definitely a right way and a wrong way to ask for private money. I'm going to save you some time and show you the right way. You need to be able to communicate to a private lender or a private funding source exactly how their funds are going to be used, how the particular deal is structured, how long it's going to take and what specifically the deal entails. Follow these tips, and you will be able to raise private money.

First of all, there are four steps to the real estate industry. We all know the steps are find a deal, fund the deal, fix the deal and then find a buyer.

How do you find private lenders to fund a real estate deal? You can use private funders who have IRAs. If, for example, you have relatives or business acquaintances who have IRAs, you know that they're probably not making money in their IRAs. They probably have their IRA money stuck in stocks or mutual funds or something of that nature.

What if you were to offer that IRA holder a 10 percent return on his money, and you were able to use it to make 30 percent per year flipping houses or investing in asset-based lending or oil and gas or something else, like Forex? It could be any investment type.

Borrowing funds from other people and having them loan it from their IRA to you works great. What happens is their IRA loans your IRA the money. It's done every day.

Speed of Funds

One of the strongest advantages of using private lenders is that you can get things done quickly. You need a competitive advantage when you're making investments, and speed is a huge advantage. If you're able to get funds immediately, then you can make a decision immediately and close on a property or any other kind of investment, for that matter, when the deal comes up.

If you have private funds available to you, you never have to let profitable deals slip away. If you're trying to find private money after you find the deal, then it's too late, because by the time you line up the money, the deal will be gone. Your goal is to find the private money first, find the people who are willing to invest in a project, and they can be ready, waiting in the wings to fund the deal when you bring it to them.

So, you want to find someone who says, "Yes. I will commit to loan you money at 8 percent interest or 10 percent interest if I'm happy with the deal you bring me." Then you go out and find the deal. If they agree to that particular deal, then you go ahead and borrow the funds. If the investor is already in place and ready to go, then you can take action immediately and pull the trigger.

Now, because most lenders prefer not to deal with monthly payments, you have an ever-increasing flow of cash to use to your advantage. Let's say you borrowed money from someone else's IRA, and you've got a one-year loan at 8 percent.

Well, that means that during that one year, if there is cash flow coming in from a rental or from flipping a house or flipping properties, you could use that money over and over and over again and not have to pay interest until the one-year term is up. Imagine if you had the use of the money for a two-year or three-year term. It's perfectly acceptable to negotiate a deal where you don't pay any interest for one year or two years. That's called a term loan, and the term loan gives you the ability to use all the money for the entire time and not have to worry about paying interest starting the first month like most regular loans. The interest is accrued and paid along with the principle at the end of the term.

We all know that when you're working deals, if you have cash up front you're going to get a better deal. That's very simple. If you are walking in with cash, you're going to be ahead of someone who has to get financing or funding from somewhere else. If you're trying to buy a short sale or a foreclosure, having cash in hand will enable you to win the house over someone else who's waiting for a loan. When you are making offers on properties, you want to have your private funding already available. Let your sellers know that you have cash ready to go. You are much more likely to get the deal over someone who needs to get financing (which may or may not come through). In many cases, you can get a discount for paying all cash for a property, so you'll probably save money that way, too.

Even a couple of thousand dollars makes a big difference in the scheme of things when you're doing multiple properties like we do. Simply put, you can close more deals with cash. If you have a private funding source, you can get a deal done more quickly. The money comes in; you buy the house quickly; you flip it quickly and do it again. Obviously, there's no down payment, no prepayment penalties and reduced closing costs. All of this comes into play when you're using cash. By paying cash, everything goes faster and more smoothly.

You Control the Deal

Remember, if you're using private money, there are no points to pay on the loan as you would with a mortgage broker or a hard money lender. You make the rules. For the first time, you'll be in control. You have the ability to negotiate the deal with the private source the way you want it. If you need the money for a year, then ask for a year, and if you need the money for two years, then ask for two years. The idea, though, is that you are in control, and you can set the parameters and negotiate any loan terms that you want as long as they are agreeable to the other party.

You want to keep your lenders happy. We use generous terms with our lenders so they're willing to do business with us, in fact, happy to do business with us. If you pay someone 10 percent interest, that makes them happy. They will come back for that. Where else can they find 10 percent interest on solid, earning properties? It's very difficult to find. Therefore, by offering them generous terms, they will be happy and they will continue to loan you money.

If you always try to get the cheapest rate and try to offer lenders 5 percent or 6 percent, they are not going to be impressed. They can put their money into other things like bonds and annuities and not have to worry about any risk or any loss of control. If they're going to give up control of some of their money to you, then you should definitely reward them with the higher interest rate of 10 or 11 percent, give or take, and that will keep your investors coming back and giving you more money.

When I have private funding sources, I am 100 percent ready at any time to take advantage of any deal that comes my way. Because of their involvement, it gives me the ability to pull the trigger on any kind of foreclosure, bank-owned property or other investments, like oil and gas or Forex or asset-based lending. I can pull the trigger on an investment immediately without having to try to scrape up the money at the last minute or try to borrow it from somebody. That could take too long and you can miss out on great opportunities. Always have the money ready to go when the time is ready for the investment.

Finding Private Lenders

How do you find a lender? How do you find someone with an IRA or someone who has money, for that matter? There are a lot of ways to do it, but obviously, family members are the first place to check. If you look through all of your family members, you may find that some of them are working at companies and have an old 401(k) plan from a previous company, or they might have an IRA sitting somewhere with $5,000 in it or even $2,000. Whatever it is, it can be used to control properties, real estate or anything, really. Check with family members first, and again, if a brother or sister could loan you money, that's the easiest way. If not, you can check with cousins and more distant relatives or neighbors, good friends, etc.

Newspaper ads are another way to find lenders. It can be very simple: "Looking for Private Money," and, "High return, safe investment." Put newspaper ads in. You can do the same thing with flyers or use online classified sites such as Craigslist.org. Craigslist is free. You can advertise for private money on Craigslist. You can advertise for private money anywhere on the Internet and probably get some results as long as you're consistent about it.

You can put out flyers at different investment groups. In your town where you live or within an hour's drive, there are probably several investment groups. Some of them are real estate investment groups. Others are just general investment groups or venture capital groups. If you attend these different kinds of groups, then you would probably end up meeting new people, shaking hands and building rapport, eventually asking them if they would invest with you. You should definitely attend every kind of real estate club or function or any other kind of networking groups that you can.

Seminars are another great place to find private lenders. What about a seminar where there's a speaker there and there are many students in the room or many potential customers in the room? A lot of the people who attend a real estate seminar are investors who have money, but maybe they don't have time to do the investment on their own. Maybe they would rather trust you with their money and get a good return and not have to deal with the actual physical buying or selling of a property or an investment.

We're talking about networking, word of mouth and then all the other forms of advertising that you are aware of. The internet is going to be one of your biggest and fastest methods of finding private money. In addition to online classified ad sites, you can use social media such as Facebook and Twitter. Posting what you do on Facebook and other social networking sites will give you exposure. You never know where the investor is going to come from.

If you were to do a wide range of marketing this way, through newspapers, flyers, social media and going to face-to-face events, you will be able to find people who will loan you money, as long as you can prove to them that both you as a person and the investment are a safe bet.

First, find private money. Someone has it; it's out there. Then find the investment, and then convince them that it's a safe bet to invest in you.

Obviously, the major benefit of having private money ready is so you can purchase a property immediately when a good deal comes up. The funding is available at all times; and it gives you better cash flow. If you can access private funds that can be used to buy rental properties and have 10 rental properties or 20 or 50, with monthly payments coming in and you don't have to pay the lender until the end of the year or the end of two years, you can quickly build up your cash flow and your profits.

The point is, by having private money you can leverage yourself and grow 10 times faster, especially if you're doing it tax-free in a Roth IRA. Using your Roth IRA creates a significant, significant difference in growing your wealth.

Here are some advantages for using private money. Let's use real estate, for example. Ready available cash allows you to buy real estate fast and buy it at a discount. You don't need to go through the process of the credit check. You don't need to qualify. You're not going to a bank to borrow the money. Your credit is really irrelevant in this case, and since most people have bad credit, getting private money is probably the only way to find money in this day and age. There's no credit check, and it does not show up on your credit report.

Let's say you get a loan from a brother or sister or some acquaintance of yours or a business partner. That particular loan does not show up on your credit report, which means that it does not reduce your credit score and does not take away from your borrowing power if you should need your credit to borrow some money for some other reason. Therefore, it does not decrease your score whatsoever, and it does not show up on the radar. It's not even noticeable anywhere. This gives you access to basically unlimited funds. If you have private money, you are at a huge advantage because you have as much money as you could possibly need to continue to do deals as long as the investor is protected.

If the investor is protected, then they don't worry about the risk. If for some reason the deal doesn't work, you want to show them that you still have an exit strategy to get them paid back, That's what you need to convince them of: How they will be paid back if the property doesn't sell at a profit. At that point, you would sell it at break-even and pay back the investor.

The idea is that you need to be sure that you have all your bases covered so that you can convince the private investor that it's safe to bet on you, and it's safe to bet on the investment you picked. If you can convince them of that, then they will be open to investing in more deals with you and continue to send either more money or let you reuse the same money over and over and over again.

When you do this, you can negotiate the terms that you want. The advantage is you set the rules. You decide when you pay them back. You negotiate the interest rate. You negotiate the time when you return their money, and if it works, if it's a win-win, then the deals get done. But remember: Make it a win-win. Don't fight over the interest rate when you can make more by using the money. I'll give you an example.

Would I pay 13, 14 or 15 percent for private money with no points? Absolutely. If I can make 30 percent on my money doing something with it, why wouldn't I pay 15 percent to a lender if I had to?

If that was my only choice, and I could not get the money at 8, 9 or 10 percent, I would do it for 15 percent. I have no problem with going ahead and paying the 15 percent at the end of the year or two years, doing the investments and still making money without using my own money.

The other advantage, as we said, is cash flow. If you have borrowed money from someone else, and you have a rental property or any other kind of cash flow from other investments like asset-based lending or oil and gas, now you're getting cash flow every single month or every quarter or whatever the term is, and that money can be used to not only grow but to pay back the lender, as well.

You have flexibility. Your money from a private investor will be there and accessible with his or her permission when you have a deal. Even if you're pre-approved by a bank, the process for some reason always has to start fresh, involving re-approval, an appraisal (sometimes two) and the time-consuming underwriting process. With a private lender, you have some flexibility where you're not under the gun to purchase something within a certain amount of time or lose the deal.

One of the other advantages of using private money is that it does help your friends and family, whoever loaned you the money. If your lender can make better returns of 8 to 10 percent instead of zero to 4 percent, then everybody wins.

Think of all the family and friends you might have who are only earning five percent return or eight percent return or losing money. If they put it with you, loaned it to you or your IRA, then you would pay them back an interest rate that would probably beat whatever they're currently making.

It's not that difficult to show someone that they're making 5 percent now, and if they invest with you, they can make 9 or 10 percent. It's a matter of showing them what you're going to do with the money, finding out what they're currently earning on their money and showing them that what you have is better. It may take some convincing, so you need to prepare what you are going to say so you can explain it to them in a way that they feel safe.

You get to meet a lot of good people. When you're going to investment groups and investment seminars like I do constantly, you're meeting all kinds of good people, potential investors, potential friends, potential family, and to me, I think it's worth it, because it really does grow your whole network. Remember, it's not what you know, it's who you know. Networking with people who have money is a goldmine. Always, always, always look for investors, even if you don't currently have a deal.

As a matter of fact, my whole purpose every day and all day is to always find more investors, because all of us eventually run out of money when we invest our own money. In order to grow further, you have to go out and meet new people. You have to attend every function possible and build more potential investors to partner with on deals.

Upfront Profits and Greater Profits

Don't forget, when using private money, you can get profits when you buy. There are ways to purchase something and make a profit right from the very beginning and get paid right away, even though your loan isn't due for one year or two years.

If you've made a profit in 30 days of $30,000, you can easily continue to go ahead and use the funds, because you have a one-year loan. That's awesome. Now, you have profits immediately, and you have the ability to go ahead and reuse the money. You can also make offers in confidence when you have money sitting there on the sidelines, because you know that you can close the deal.

When you have money ready to go, sitting on the sidelines from a private investor, you can feel very confident in making aggressive offers and saying, "Look, I have cash. Here's the proof. Let's make a deal." It's easy to construct profitable exit strategies. It's easy to construct deals when you have cash and things are ready to go.

It also saves you money. In fact, if you are trying to consummate a deal, and you have cash available, it might save you money in closing costs. It might save you money on any points or any lending fees. It could save you money on the actual purchase price of the property.

There are tons of advantages to doing it this way. The way the economy is now, with lending tight, no banks lending any money, probably the most effective way to grow your wealth right now is to use other people's IRAs that can loan your IRA money, and you can make money tax-free. That is a great way to finance anything, deals, projects, businesses. Right now, the IRA and 401(k) plan is the secret to getting things done. We have to self-fund. We have to use our own monies to fund deals rather than waste time trying to work with banks that are not able to loan money anymore.

Cheaper than a Partner

Remember that when you find a private investor and you borrow money from him the advantage is that it's much cheaper than taking on a partner. If you took on a partner with the money, you might share 50 percent of the deal with them. If someone brings you the money, and you have to give them 50 percent of the deal, that's a heck of a lot more than paying 10 percent interest or 12 percent interest or 15 percent interest. Using private money is much cheaper than taking on a partner. You are way better off with private money because you have control.

You can fund purchases of performing or non-performing notes. You don't even have to take over a property. You can easily buy real estate, just the notes, using private money and not have to physically take over the asset itself.

You can even lend money that someone loaned you. Let's say that you borrowed money at 8 percent interest, and you were able to loan it out at 12 percent interest to someone else. Any set of numbers works as long as you are borrowing at the lower rate and loaning out the money at the higher rate. The key is to use the spread to your advantage and make money that way. By borrowing money and using it to make more money, it's going to give you an edge, rather than just relying on your $5,000 a year contribution.

No Credit Issues

When you have cash, there's no credit check and no credit report. That solves that problem. With private money, credit problems are no longer a problem. You can still buy houses for cash while cleaning up your credit. Credit is just not an issue when you're dealing with private money. Private money has nothing to do with your credit and your credit doesn't matter. Anybody with poor credit can borrow private funds from a private individual in their IRA, use it to make money and clean up your credit over time. It will pay to get those credit issues straightened out when the banks finally do start lending again, whenever that may be.

Remember, private lenders don't ask about your credit report, and they don't go to the credit agencies. The people who are looking to loan based on your credit score are not the people you're looking for, because your credit has nothing to do with your ability to pay. If your credit is bad, that does not automatically mean that you're a bad payer. It may mean that you lost your job. It may mean that you were overextended because of too many real estate deals or because the bank allowed you to borrow that much money. Not having good credit is not an issue. You want to find a person who does not rely on your credit report as a reason to loan you money. A private individual is not measuring your credit. Private lenders want to know, "What's the risk, when can I get my money back and what interest rate will I get?" Very simple.

With private lenders, you can borrow unlimited amounts of money on your terms. You can borrow as much as you want without having to worry about the terms that the bank gives you. Remember, with the banks, they're setting specific terms. You've got to pay monthly, you have to pay this rate, you can only borrow so much or have mortgages on a limited number of properties. With private money, you can continue to borrow private money, and there's no limit. You can borrow $1 million, $2 million, $5 million, $10 million. You can continue to find private money if you market for it as I am about to show you.

You also maintain control. When you're investing and using private money, the private money person who lent you the money is not trying to tell you how to run the investment or not trying to tell you what to do. You maintain all the control. You decide when to buy, when to sell or what to do with the investment. No one else steers you or guides you when you're borrowing private money. You also decide who to work with and who not to work with and you decide the terms.

If you don't have a job but you have a deal, would a bank loan you money? No. But, could you still borrow private money even if you didn't have a full-time job and you were just an investor?

Absolutely. With the bank, you're going to need a down payment, you need good credit, and sometimes, it takes four to five months to close a deal because of the underwriting process. With cash, you can go in and buy immediately. If you're using a bank, you're going to lose time and sometimes even lose a deal.

Typically, you don't build a good relationship with a bank. It's just an entity that you're doing business with, and therefore, they don't care about you as a private money person would. In addition, banks are constantly changing the rules. They can decrease the amount of your credit line. They can take your credit line away. They can change the interest rate. They can take it away from you or stop allowing you to use the money for any reason at all, unfortunately.

It's not a good idea to use banks for investing. The banks require, of course, a lot of paperwork. They require you to show your credit report. You've got to provide a stack of documents, which is a pain in the neck, and jump through all their hoops. You don't have any control of anything at all, and you have to make monthly payments, which is definitely a detriment.

There are some problems with hard money lenders. First of all, the hard money lenders are very expensive. They do charge points and that could be expensive. They typically check your credit, and since a lot of people have bad credit that cuts a lot of people out of the hard money borrower pool.

Typically, a hard money lender will require that you put a down payment on the house before they give you any money at all. They want you to have some "skin in the game." Rather than getting 100 percent of the money, you might only get 50 percent of the money. And you're only allowed one exit strategy; that is to sell for cash. They will not allow you to hold a property using the hard money.

Hard money is only for short term, usually for three or four months. Quite honestly, if you hold a property long term, you're not making any money if the hard money lender charges you the rates they normally do. A hard money lender might charge you three to five points and anywhere from 10 to 15 percent, which gets very expensive fast. If you can borrow money without points and maybe at 8, 9 or 10 percent interest at the most, you'll be fine.

You remember, too, that a hard money lender may not even loan you money for the rehab. They might say, "Well, we'll give you money for the purchase, but the $10,000 or $15,000 or $20,000 in rehab, you'll have to pay on your own. You're limited in what you can do with a hard money lender. That leads us back to the obvious point that a private lender is the way to go. Private lenders, especially those with IRAs and old 401(k) plans, have billions of dollars sitting in those plans that can be used to loan to your IRA.

What about using a line of credit? Again, a line of credit is going to require that you make monthly payments, and you're limited to the amount of the line of credit. Also, lines of credit can be cut or closed at any time and you don't have any control.

What about using your own money and your own credit cards? First, you're limited to what money you really have, and that runs out. With credit cards, you could borrow money at interest rates that are astronomical, and if you miss one payment, all of a sudden, the rates go up to 22 to 25 percent or more, and now, the amount of money that you're paying out on interest eats up all your profit or puts you in a loss position. We don't suggest that you use credit cards.

Marketing for Private Money

If you can use private money instead of your own cash, you're going to have a lot more buying power. To get the word out, to start to attract these private lenders, you're going to want to go to as many one-on-one meetings as you can with acquaintances and people to explain what you're trying to accomplish.

People nowadays are so used to giving and getting business cards that it's almost to the point where it's overkill, and people just throw the business cards out. You need to stand out, to do something different. One idea is to record a short, five- minute audio or video and put it on a CD or a DVD. You can hand that out and give it to people almost like your business card.

You're presenting a polished package. You want to get people's attention by looking professional and by being different from everyone else. When you're meeting private lenders for the first time, instead of handing them an ordinary business card, give them your CD or DVD that has your short presentation on it, and don't forget to put your contact information on there, as well.

You want to make sure that the outside of the cover has your company name on it, the logo, your contact information, everything that's necessary including your website and email address. It's a great idea to have testimonials on there. If they never pop the CD or DVD in the player, they will still probably read a testimonial or two. Testimonials are awesome for your short audio or video business card. Remember, too, that when you hand out a DVD or CD, put your regular business card in there, as well, in case they want to scan it and put you in their database.

You could even mail your audio business card to potential lenders. What I would do is take your audio or DVD and mail it to a potential investor so that he can listen to it for a couple of minutes and see who you are and what you do.

You can give them away at your one-to-one luncheons. I'm going to talk about doing luncheon presentations a bit later in this chapter. For now, know that when you have a luncheon where you have 30 people there, give each person a CD or DVD. It's good to give them away to people one at a time, when you meet them face-to-face. Make sure that everyone gets one. It will help get your message across so that people will begin to take you seriously and trust you.

Direct Mail

You can do a direct mail campaign to potential investors and send them mail consistently saying, "Invest with me. Invest with me. I'm a safe bet. I give 10 percent interest. Call my office to hear more details." Not those words, of course, but that is the underlying message that you want to send. "Invest with me. I know what I am doing. I pay high rates."

Television and Radio

You could even use a TV commercial. You could use spots on television, if you wanted to, to find private money. The same thing goes for radio commercials. The idea is get the word out. You've got to ask for private money to get it. It's not going to just come to you. You have to do marketing to find private money, just as you would to find a deal.

A Few More Marketing Pointers

Another way to market and build your credibility at the same time is by using newspaper articles. Many papers will let you have a weekly or monthly column (sometimes in exchange for advertising). When people read something you have written in a newspaper, it gives you an expert status which gives you immediate credibility.

You can also do different kind of presentations. You can easily put together a PowerPoint presentation. The benefit of a PowerPoint presentation is that now they're actually hearing you and seeing you. If you put together a presentation using PowerPoint, it should have the details about what you do with the money, how long you've been doing it and what returns you can provide to them and how you plan to pay them back.

Also, if someone does loan you money, and you return and pay them back in a timely manner, you should get a testimonial recording from them. You would record them for a minute and let them tell about how you did a great job on returning their money on time and that you paid them the money you promised to pay them, and that they were very satisfied and so on. Testimonials are very powerful and effective in building credibility. If you were to get those testimonials on video or even a written text testimonial, it will be very, very advantageous for you. This will allow people to trust you sooner rather than later.

One-on-One Meetings

When you're calling someone to meet with them one-to-one to discuss the investment and lending, you want to set a date for the meeting suitable for both people, obviously. Make sure they are not rushed for time and that the two of you have set aside enough time for you to properly make your presentation. Prepare your presentation ahead of time. Have all the details ready to go so that there are no questions left over. Make a checklist, not just for materials that you are going to use in your presentation, but a checklist of what you are going to say. Have another checklist of "Frequently Asked Questions" that covers questions that most investors have. Questions like, "How is my money secured?" "What interest rate will you pay?" "When do I get my money back?" Make sure you have everything on the checklist ready to go.

Be sure you arrive on time. The way to do that is to make sure you're there a few minutes early and that you're set up with everything ready to go. Make sure you have studied your materials.

Look professional. Wear a suit. Women, same thing: Wear a suit. Look sharp. Make sure that you look credible, professional, and that you look trustworthy. Make your presentation and then ask them to invest with you.

That last sentence was key. Don't make a presentation and NOT ask for the money. Just say, "Hey, look. I'd like you to go ahead and give us a try." Without asking for the order or asking for the money, you're not going to get it. You want to make sure you ask them to go ahead and loan you the funds based on the materials that you gave them.

Luncheon Presentations

One of the ways that I've been able to raise private money is to hold lunch events or even a cocktail event. If you hold a lunch event for 30 or 40 business acquaintances or 30 or 40 friends, you can then make a simple five or ten minute presentation and explain to them that you borrow private money and you pay out 10 percent interest or whatever it is. Tell them you're looking for investors to invest with you and that you can then get them a better return than what they're getting on their money now. By doing those private luncheons or events like that, you will not only mingle with them, but build rapport, build integrity, build credibility. As you have these and have them often, you will build good friendships with people who will take a chance on you, trust you and give you a try.

Remember, when you're doing a luncheon, you're speaking to 30 people at one time or 20 people at one time. This is a great way to leverage your time. The idea is to speak to 20 or 30 people at a time -- get your message out to them, instead of talking to one person at a time.

Find a good meeting location. Pick a nice restaurant where you can use a back room that holds 30 or 40 people. That's always one of the best places. You need to make sure you control the atmosphere, that there are no interruptions. You should have the waitress take your orders and then ask the waitress to not come back in for about 20 or 30 minutes while you make your presentation. When you're finished giving your presentation, the waitress comes back in and serves the food for everybody.

Always have a controlled atmosphere where you're the one in charge. Make sure there are no other interruptions, whether it's in a private room at a restaurant or your personal residence, for that matter. You need an environment that is controlled, quiet, where everyone will have a chance to listen to you.

Another advantage to talking to groups is that you can answer everyone's questions at once. Let's say someone asks you a question, like, "How long have you been doing this?" Well, when you answer the question, you're answering it in front of 30 other people. It makes everyone feel more comfortable if the questions are getting asked all together. It really does provide credibility more quickly.

So, why a luncheon or why a cocktail party or something like that? Easy. There's no pressure. Everybody's happy, having fun. It's really low-key and no stress involved. It's very professional. You can linger, mingle with people and get to know them a little better and vice versa. A lot of people in the room will have synergy with you and have some of the same interests in mind and may end up loaning you lots and lots of money. It's just a matter of being persistent. It does work.

And then of course, you must follow up. When these people attend your functions or see your materials, you have to call them back and continuously spend time with them and build a rapport with them until the transaction does take place. You've got to follow up with everybody.

I like to use what we call an "Indication of Interest" form. It's just a form to fill out, a little questionnaire that says that "Are you interested in loaning funds? Have you done this before? How much do you have to loan? Where is it coming from? Is it in an IRA or a 401(k) plan?" This gives your audience, the people in the room, a chance to respond.

You can use the form to see if your presentation was effective. For example, you might want to ask the question "Was the presentation informative? What did you not understand?" If you could find out what the people in the room did not understand or what they don't feel comfortable with by doing a little quiz at the end of the presentation, you can fix whatever is wrong. This form will help determine your luncheon success, and it will determine whether your attendees take action and loan you the money or not. You definitely want to find out what they're thinking and then also, do they have funds to loan you, have they done this before and do they like what they heard?

Here's what would go on the interest form besides the questions I mentioned to you. Of course, their contact information: Name, address, phone number and e-mail, and maybe if you want to get any other information, like their Facebook account. You want to find out their decision. Have they decided to go forward? What are they going to do? Are they yes, in? Are they on the fence? Are they hot, cold? What are they feeling? How are they feeling about it?

Don't miss a chance to ask for referrals. There may be people in the room who might not have enough funds to loan you or maybe didn't feel comfortable with the investment, but they may know someone who would. Maybe they have a family or a friend or somebody else who would happily take the interest rate you offered.

Ask how much they are willing to loan to you. Will they lend you $5,000, $10,000, $50,000? What is the amount that they feel comfortable with after hearing everything from you? Definitely, all this would go on the interest form. You want to have them fill it out, turn it back into you, so you can figure out exactly how you did, good, bad or indifferent. I have provided a sample Indication of Interest form for you at the end of this section.

Once you have met these people for lunch or a cocktail party, you want to make sure you follow up, and of course, sending a thank-you note is number one. Handwrite it out, use a card or a letter, and send it with a stamp.

Make sure that you write a personal thank you, not a generic one. Handwrite it, sign it and mean it. Put a special note to each person in there. "Tom, I really liked talking to you. I enjoyed finding out more about your family. I look forward to working with you. Thanks for attending my luncheon." It's got to be handwritten. Don't send it on your computer. Don't send an e-mail out saying thank you. Send a handwritten card in the mail. That's the only way to go.

It's critical to make sure that you show you're a professional and show that you really care, and that builds trust and rapport. If you decide to wait and not contact these people right after the event, you'll probably lose their interest.

The very next day after your presentation, you need to contact these people one by one and really find out what level of interest they have, using the forms they have filled out. Those forms are going to help you a great deal.

How do you group the attendees? Some of the attendees will want to loan money and want to know the facts. Other attendees just want more information. You can separate the people into two different groups, where one group is only learning about lending money and they're not really at the point to actually lend money yet. That's okay. That works. The second group is made up of the people who are actually ready to lend, they are ready to get involved. Separate your attendees into these two groups.

Sometimes, there are people who cannot attend, they can't make it to the luncheon, but they still want information. Go ahead and mail them the information. Send them whatever you possibly can to show them what you're doing and how you're doing it and how you're going to pay them back. Anybody who did not show up, anybody who could not make it, send them the information. Some of those people may end up referring other people to you. Go ahead and mail out your information to those people as well.

Do Not Call List

If someone is on a do-not-call list, then you don't contact them by phone. It's that simple. However, you do want to make sure your Indication of Interest form contains the following:

"By providing the above information, you are consenting to receive phone calls from our group about our services." It's just a simple line with those words or words to that effect.

You want to make sure you have something in writing that allows you to call these people. You don't want them to say, "Hey, look, why are you calling me? I'm on the do-not-call list." If you get an agreement from them saying that you're allowed to call them, that protects you.

Keep a call log, as well, to make sure that you're tracking who you called and keep good notes on it. Most importantly, respect people's wishes. If they don't want a phone call, then don't call them. Send them an e-mail, send them something by regular mail. Whatever it is they want, make sure you follow their wishes.

The type of people that you don't want to work with are the ones who are going to evaluate everything you do, tell you what to do and get in the way of the process. You don't want someone telling you how much to pay for a property or how much to repair a property for or what price to sell it at. That's all done by you. You want to make sure that you do not have someone who is going to tell you what to do or run your deal. That will never work. If they want to be involved in a process, you've got the wrong lender.

If someone wants to loan you a great deal of money and it's much more than you need, then that's not going to help you any. You want to find someone who's going to loan you the right amount of money. If they want to loan you $5 million, and you only have use for $100,000, then that's the wrong person for you, tempting as it is.

Most people ask the question, "Well, what if you need more money?" For example, you run into extra costs while rehabbing a house. Some of the investors won't want you to mingle the money. If that happens, you just need to make sure you keep the money separate. The money may come from you for the rehab and the investor for the purchase. That's one way to do it. Or there are other ways to go ahead and get the job done.

Creating Mortgages

If you are using money from two sources on one project, you definitely need to create mortgages. The private lender with more cash gets first mortgage. For example, if one lender is loaning you money for the house, and the other lender is loaning you money for the repairs, then you would have two mortgages. The first lien goes to the person who put up the most money. The second mortgage or lien goes to the person who put up the lesser amount of money. It's very simple. The mortgages are put on the property to protect your investors.

Rules for Private Lending

There are some rules you need to know about for private lending.

Loan Minimum and Maximum Limits. When you borrow money from somebody, you want to make sure that you know what the minimum amount is that they'll allow you to use and what the maximum amount is that they'll allow you to use.

Make interest payments when property sells. You want to make sure that the interest payment is made when the property sells, not on a monthly basis. You want the interest due and payable upon the sale of the property. That's the best way to do it.

One lender per promissory note. You don't want to have several lenders on one note. On your promissory note, only have one at a time on there to avoid confusion.

Seventy percent loan to value. If you tell your lender that you will not pay more than 70% of the value of the property (for example, sales price plus rehab and carrying costs) make sure you keep your word and that you don't go over what you agreed. Only borrow up to what they are giving you for that property.

Do not take the money directly. Always have the money sent to your attorney so there's no potential comingling of the funds. You want to make sure that the check goes right to your attorney's escrow account.

Use Mortgages. Once the actual money comes in to your attorney's account, make sure that you issue mortgages on that property so that the lender is safe and protected.

If someone loans you $100,000 to buy a property, you want to make sure that you put a mortgage on the house so that the lender is protected in case of a default or in case of a potential problem. Always put a mortgage on the property so that the lender is covered as a first lien holder.

Specify when the payments start and when the payments end. For example, if you have a one-year term, then make sure it's specified in the agreement that it will be paid at the end of one year.

Put the Terms in Writing. Be sure that all of the rules and all of the agreements are specified in the contract and nothing is left out. That's critical.

CONCLUSION

Struggling to find money will always slow down your wealth building. The key is to grow your wealth by borrowing funds from many other IRAs and many other 401(k) plans that you can put into your self-directed IRA to do deals with. For me, I was able to borrow lots and lots of money from other people's IRAs over the years, which allowed me to grow my portfolio. That made a significant difference, because had I not done that, I would have had to rely on my contribution, which is $5,000 a year. That's not going to make you wealthy. It's not enough to make a big enough difference.

You need to spend time looking for private money, and believe me, it's out there. The reality is that about half of the people that you know have an IRA or old 401(k) plan. How do you know? You ask. In a room full of 50 people anywhere, half the room will have money in their IRA or a 401(k) plan of some sort to potentially lend to you. It is a big market.

A lot of people have money that you don't even know have any money. The only way to find out is to say to them, "Do you have an IRA or old 401(k) plan?" If they say yes, then say, "Would you be interested in looking at a deal and looking at loaning me money to invest with me? I pay good rates. I pay high rates." If they say yes, then you've got a potential customer, potential lender, and you should definitely pursue that.

Without consistent and adequate funding, you don't get any deals done. You've got to have money constantly to use to get ahead in life. No matter what it's for, whether it's for real estate or any other investment strategy, you've got to have access to other people's funds that you borrow and you pay back on time. Private money is your key to getting ahead.

Indication of Interest Form

Thank you so much for helping us by filling out this brief questionnaire. We want to make sure our presentations are informative and thorough.

Was the presentation informative? Did you come away with a clear understanding of how my program works?

_____

What did you not understand or what did you find confusing?

_____

Have you ever loaned funds privately before? Y/N

Would you like to find out more about becoming involved in my private lenders program? Y/N

Do you currently have funds in an IRA or 401(k) that are earning less than 6% per year? Y/N

If you were to become involved in this program, how much money would you like to invest?

$5,000 – 20,000 $50,000 – 100,000

$20,000 - $50,000 $100,000 or more

Contact Information*:

Name:

Address:

City, State Zip

Phone number :   Best time to reach you:

e-mail address:

Do you know anyone who would be interested in receiving information from us on our private lending program?

Name

Address

City, State Zip

Phone number

Name

Address

City, State Zip

Phone number

*By providing the above information, you are consenting to receive phone calls from our group about our services.

APPENDIX

EPILOGUE

12 Real Estate Mistakes

Okay, we've all done it. Anyone who invests in real estate is bound to make a clunker deal sooner or later. I've been in this business for over 20 years and have made plenty of mistakes, and I am always reminded that experience is what you get right *after* you needed it.

The popularity of real estate investing has exploded in the last few years, and the media is full of war stories from new investors who find themselves in deals with problems.

In almost every case, the cause is traceable to a lack of knowledge about a few simple precepts that form the ground rules of successful real estate investments. These are the basic practices that when used correctly will eliminate the most common causes of a bad deal.

Aside from reading as many books and listening to as many tapes that I can on Real Estate investing, I also attend many conferences and boot camps.

My goal when I get to these conferences and boot camps is to seek out people who are more successful than myself and see what information I can learn from them to increase my own success.

When talking to these individuals, there is one question that I always ask and am most interested to hear their response.

That question is this:

"What was the biggest mistake you made when you first started investing and, looking back, what could you have done to avoid it?"

This question usually invokes a queer smile as these now-successful investors look back into their once unstable past and conjure up their biggest folly. Often times, they would not mention just one situation but two or three.

The biggest single quality that each of these investors possess is that when they were confronted with adversity they did not fold up their tent and decide that real estate investing was not for them. Instead, they stuck it out and turned each one of their mistakes into a valuable lesson not to be repeated.

The Japanese have a saying: "Fall down six times, get up seven." With almost every situation in life, whether it be business, family, relationships, and/or money, if you adopt this attitude, you will become unstoppable.

The following mistakes are the most common responses that I received when I asked successful investors to talk about their past.

Read them, study them and, most importantly, do not forget them. Anybody can receive information, it is the wise man who puts it to use and thereby prospers by it.

Mistake 1: Not Knowing the Four Principals

Your have probably heard that there are three principals to real estate investing (i.e., "Location, Location, Location"). If you have been involved in any decision regarding the purchase or sale of real estate, you must be aware of the importance that "location" has in these decisions.

These three real estate principals generally apply to people looking to purchase and occupy their own home (residential, owner-occupied homes). Buying your home is not real estate investing, but rather it's a necessity of life. Everyone has to live somewhere. That's why "location" is so important.

However, I found out the hard way that these three principals don't necessarily apply to investing in income producing and/or commercial properties.

If you want to invest in any type of income-producing property, then there are **four real estate principals** that must be followed:

Location   Timing

Demographics   Cash Flow

The term "**Location**" refers to a number of key factors related to the physical location of the subject property.

For example, residential properties should ideally be located in areas where there is easy access to all the basic necessities like electricity, telephone, clean water, gas, etc. Amenities like schools, hospitals, churches, grocery stores or shopping malls in the vicinity are a plus. This includes good roads and/or transportation to these amenities. And, make sure your property is not in a flood zone. You will find that these "location" factors are all interrelated and interdependent.

If you are buying the property for renting purposes, then you must also look into the demand of houses in that specific area. Some undesirable property or people in the neighborhood may also raise eyebrows. And, while it's good to have a residential property in the inner-city (not outer reaches), buying a house on an overly-crowded road or too near a congested shopping mall can backfire because of noise and all the hustle (a possible safety issue for kids).

On the other hand, commercial properties should be located at some swarming place for businesses. Transportation and parking facilities are other things to look at. If you already have some business in mind, you can see if the place attracts your potential customers (e.g. targeted age group or income class) for your business. Also make sure that you are not going for a place where plenty of other businesses are already offering the exact products or services. If the property needs lots of renovation before it can be utilized, then keep those expenditures in mind when settling on a price.

The surrounding crime rate is another important factor for both residential and commercial properties. Investors who are looking for long-term investment can earn huge profits by investing in some area going through major re-development or infrastructure programs. Buying a piece of property in this area when the work has just begun will be comparatively inexpensive, hence offering huge profit margins.

Apart from these basic "location" factors, you should consider your personal likes and dislikes about the neighborhood when finalizing a deal to invest in real estate.

The term "**Demographics**" refers to the demographic profile of the neighborhood and/or the surrounding area. You can easily get this information online from the Census data, or most school districts will post this data online or you can simply ask a local real estate agent.

The key demographic information includes: Population, number of housing units, owner-occupied housing units, renter-occupied housing units, vacant housing units, household size, household income, median age, gender, race and ethnicity. Demographics can tell you a lot about the neighborhood. Instead of looking at the "data" itself, I prefer to look at demographic "trends." For example, in the past 10 years, if the surrounding area is growing in population, vacancies are down and median income is up, then this indicates that the area is desirable. Obviously, if the trends are all down, then this indicates that something may be happening that needs further investigation. Find out why before you buy.

The term "**Timing**" refers to market conditions when you purchase your property. Before you invest in real estate, take a moment to look at local market conditions. Is the local market experiencing a housing bubble, is it in a recession, or is it holding steady? Market timing can make you a lot of money in real estate or it can leave you holding the bag. So, be sure you understand local market conditions before you buy. Obviously, it's better to buy at the end of a recession, before housing prices begin to rise. Needless to say, it is not good to buy during a housing bubble. More likely than not, you will lose. It's much better to simply wait for the market to adjust.

The term "**Cash Flow**" refers to the amount of cash coming in relative to the amount going out. Cash flow is one of the most important considerations investors face when making real estate purchases, particularly now that so many markets across the country are struggling. While "appreciation" is often the most significant form of profit for real estate investors, cash flow is easier to determine and lower risk.

Although many elements combine to influence cash flow, one of the most important ones is the surrounding market. Areas with lower home prices are more likely to have positive cash flow. Remember, there are four possible financial benefits to investing in real estate:

(1) Appreciation   (3) Tax Savings

(2) Positive Cash Flow   (4) Mortgage Amortization

Many investors expect to get most of their return from **appreciation.** Consequently, they are willing to accept little or no cash flow or more commonly, **negative** cash flow. Tax savings were drastically curtailed by the Tax Reform Act of 1986. Amortization (pay down) of the mortgage is a pittance in the early years of a loan.

I do **not** agree with the notion that you should accept negative cash flow because appreciation will more than pay you back. But that is why most investors **do** accept negative cash flow.

In fact, owning rental property almost invariably has the exact **opposite** effect on your cash flow. It takes your **current** annual cash flow and **confiscates** part of it to feed the rental property. Negative-cash-flow properties are called "alligators" because you have to feed them constantly or else they will eat you alive.

Only if you buy on a **bargain** basis or **increase the value of the property** significantly can you get positive cash flow from a rental property. Can that be done? Absolutely. Is it easy money? No. Is it **passive** income in the sit-in-a-hammock sense of that word? Hell, no! You will earn every penny of it. If you do not want to work hard and take risks, get out of real estate altogether before you get badly burned.

My Dad always told me that the secret to investing in real estate is to make your profit when you purchase the property. The only way you can do that is to buy the property below market value.

How are you going to do that?

Perhaps you have looked at six (maybe 10 deals) and you are finding it nearly impossible to make them cash flow based on collecting a reasonable rent and getting 30 year fixed rate financing.

Take a deep breath. This is one of the most common problems for real estate investors and probably one of the top things that discourages many people from starting a lucrative real estate investing business. There is hope though. Read on.

First, unless you happen to be lucky enough to live in or near a city that has a low income area where you can still buy "rental houses" where the values are about 100 times the monthly rent, you need to realize that finding these deals is like the Easter Egg hunts you had as a kid. You've got to look at a lot of deals to find that special one that will work for you and produce positive cash flow every month.

How many will you need to look at? It can vary, but I do not think that looking at 50 is out of the range of possibility.

Are you kidding? So, I need to look at 50 houses to find one that will work? Yes, you might need to look at 50 houses, making better distinctions about what might work and what will not work to find a good deal.

You may also find that putting out marketing to find motivated sellers makes finding these types of houses easier rather than just looking at houses that are for sale by owner or listed with a real estate agent.

Buying houses at a discount and/or with good terms can significantly improve your ability to make a house cash flow, especially if the interest rate on the terms you can get from a seller is much better than the current rate you could get from a bank or lender.

What if you have some houses that are very close, but none that will have positive cash flow? First, keep looking. Second, there are some ways to ethically increase the amount a tenant pays you in rent which could make a negative cash flow house a positive cash flow house.

For example, if instead of just renting the house, you sell the house on a rent-to-own plan, you can get payments that are on par with what your actual mortgage, taxes and insurance expenses are because they need to be able to pay your actual mortgage, taxes and insurance payments to afford that house.

When you interview your potential buyer, you explain that market rent is $1,000 (or whatever it is), but that if they have $10,000 to put down toward purchasing the house, their mortgage payment with taxes and insurance would be $1,400 (or whatever it is).

You tell them they need to pay the $1,400, but that you will credit the $400 above market rent toward the purchase of the house when they do go out and get their own loan and buy the house from you. In the meantime, they rent with the payment that resembles your mortgage payment and monthly expenses – thereby producing positive cash flow.

This next investment strategy is my favorite: Buy duplexes. You can buy a duplex for about the same price as a single family home. The difference is that now you have two renters paying you market price for your property. If you buy the duplex right, you should be able to pay the mortgage with the rents from one side of the duplex. The other side of the duplex pays for all other expenses. That's a great way to produce positive cash flow from day one.

For example, I recently purchased a newly constructed duplex for $200,000, which was located in a very nice subdivision. With 20% down, the mortgage payment on $160,000 loan was about $1,000. So, I rented each side of the duplex for $1,100 / month – giving me $2,200 per month of income. My taxes, insurance and miscellaneous expenses equaled about $800.00 a month. My total expenses were $1,800 a month, and with $2,200 in income, that's $400 per month in positive cash flow.

The bottom-line is: you need to look at a lot of deals to find one that will cash flow. Take your time, do your homework, and make your profit when you purchase your property. Don't put all your eggs in the "appreciation" basket.

Mistake 2: Thinking You Will Get Rich Quick

This kind of thinking is fueled by numerous "self-appointed" gurus who have television infomercials and make it sound so easy to get rich quick in real estate. To be honest, investing in real estate is not easy. My dad always told me, "There is nothing worthwhile in life that's easy. You'll have to work for it." That's especially true of real estate.

Real estate is a good long-term investment, but so is putting your money in a mutual fund, which is a lot easier. The television gurus don't talk about all that hard work and all the knowledge you'll need about real estate fundamentals. And, the gurus don't tell you that there are risks associated with investing in real estate. There is a certain risk tolerance you'll need to invest in real estate.

The bottom-line is: Investing in real estate is a good long-term investment strategy. Patience is an investment virtue. Get rich quick = get poor quick!

Mistake 3: Not Having a Plan

In my opinion, the biggest mistake real estate investors make is not having a plan. Most people know "WHY" they are getting into real estate investing, but they just don't know "HOW" to do it. A goal without an action plan is futile.

All successful real estate investors have a continuous, consistent plan of action that they follow daily. After all, real estate investing is a numbers game and daily or weekly activities are necessary to ensure the success of any real estate project.

I see people all the time buying a property because they think they got a good deal. Then, they try to figure out what to do with it. Unfortunately, that's working backwards.

The problem is that most people look at real estate as a "transaction" rather than an "investment strategy." People fall in love with a property and throw all logic out the window. I say, forget about the property and fall in love with your potential return-on-investment (which should be based on fundamentals, not on how much you love the property).

The first thing you need to do is to find a plan that works for you. Then, you find the property that fits your plan. In other words, decide on your investment strategy BEFORE you pick your property.

The fastest way to earn a million dollars in real estate investing is to have a plan. Then, and only then, you can plan your purchase, plan your renovation work, plan your maintenance, plan your leasing strategy, plan your expenses, plan your marketing and resale strategy, etc., etc., etc. A well-executed plan improves your odds of success. *If you fail to plan, you plan to fail.*

Nothing substantial in life is completed without some sort of plan. So, you must plan your real estate investing with the same philosophy. To get from where you are now to one million dollars, you have to plan to perform certain activities and meet certain milestones to get to your goal.

Without your plan constantly in mind, you will drift aimlessly and unprofitably, like a sailboat without a rudder, until you begin to sink in those shark-infested waters called foreclosure or bankruptcy.

After you start planning consistently, you will realize that anytime your business starts getting chaotic, you'll stop, pause, and realize that you have gotten away from your original plan. The fastest way to get order back into your real estate business is to begin planning again.

The bottom-line is: Use the next 30 days to find a real estate investment strategy that fits your risk tolerance. Then, and only then, start looking for the property that fits that investment strategy. Finally, stick to the plan if it's working for you. If things get chaotic, take a moment to re-assess your plan and make the necessary adjustments to get back on course.

Mistake 4: Lousy Due Diligence

Most people aren't qualified to perform open-heart surgery without years of education and training. Yet, many real estate investors don't think twice about taking their financial lives in their hands without even cracking a book or attending one seminar.

That's where a lot of real estate investors trip up. They don't do their due diligence about the transaction or the property itself. They don't really understand the costs and/or the market conditions, and they wind up draining their personal savings because the house needs extensive repairs or they can't sell it.

You need to educate yourself before you put your financial security on the line. Take the time to read articles and books about real estate investing. Or, attend several local real estate investment groups. Speakers at monthly meetings cover everything from buying foreclosures to screening tenants. If you can't find a local investment group, find out who owns a lot of rental properties in your area, call them up and offer to pay them for an hour or two of their time to find out about the best real estate investment strategies. Tell them about your plans and ask for their advice. Perhaps there are a few things you will learn from this experience that could really save you money on your next deal.

The less knowledge you have about your real estate investment, the more risk you'll end up taking. Investing blind means buying real estate as if your eyes are shut - such as blindly believing all you're told at real estate seminars or from real estate agents. You must do your research; read and read and then read some more on the subject. Ask others who have been successful and learn from them. Just a little lack of knowledge could mean that you end up with a bad purchase and deep in debt.

Don't forget that the internet is one of the greatest tools of all time for real estate investors. It is the single best place to perform due diligence. This is especially true for investors who are located in counties where the property tax rolls are available online. If your county property records are available online, you can quickly find out who owns the property, when it was purchased, how much it costs, and its value for tax assessment purposes.

Most of the time, you can instantly obtain the current owner's name and mailing address, sale price, and the dates of the most recent and previous sales, and the tax assessed value of the property broken down by land and improvements. You can also get a site map showing the improvements to the property, along with the tax account number for the property.

Many investors who perform due diligence on a property, fail to check out the property owner at the same time. You need to know as much about the property owner as possible. You need to determine if there are any unusual factors such as the bankruptcy or divorce, a judgment, criminal charges, etc., or anything else that could put you in a better bargaining position.

Google is your friend. Google is the best place to perform due diligence on a property. It's also a good idea to enter the property owner's name in Google and see what you can find out. While you're at it, you should enter the address of the property in Google. Many times you will find all the information about previous listings in the Multiple Listing Service on that particular property.

You also need to check with either the state or the local environmental authorities when purchasing a property. You certainly don't want to buy a hidden toxic waste dump. According to today's federal law, the environmental liability is shared by the new owner of the property. Ever wonder why you see so many vacant gas stations? It is because the ground underneath them has been polluted and nobody wants to buy the property and accept that liability.

When purchasing a property for investment purposes, trust no one, verify everything, and assume nothing. Don't rely on information found in the Multiple Listing Service to be true. After all, this information was provided for the sole purpose of selling the house.

The bottom-line is: If you're going to buy real estate, you have to spend time doing your due diligence on the property. If you don't, there are many ways that "unknown factors" can eat away at the potential profits, resulting in a financial loss on the transaction -- all because you failed to perform your due diligence. Don't let that happen to you.

Mistake 5: Ignoring Local Market Conditions

Speaking of lousy due diligence, there are two levels of due diligence that are absolutely required to adequately evaluate a real estate investment: (1) local market conditions and (2) the property itself. Of the two, local market conditions trump everything else.

The first level of due diligence is understanding local market conditions. A great property in a bad market can be a big loser. A poor property in a great market can be a gold mine. How do you know the difference? Know your market.

The truth is that every market is different. A unique deal technique or a particular property type that is profitable in one market does not mean the same holds true everywhere else.

Analyzing the demographic trends of population growth, income, and employment in the local market will tell you where opportunity lies, or not. It will also show which property types are in demand or in oversupply. Those conditions will make or break your investment.

Investing in an area with declining demographic trends is destined for trouble. So, learn your market. Then, listen as it tells you how, when, and where to invest.

The value of your property is often determined by local market conditions, for example: Rental rates, occupancy levels, competitive space supply, demographic trends, quality of schools, access to retail, entertainment, shopping centers, etc.

By systematically collecting just a few local demographic statistics (job growth, population growth and income levels) and property performance fundamentals, you can stay ahead of the curve. You will be able to see trends coming rather than trying to catch the last one, thereby creating your own opportunities and reducing your vulnerability to competitive projects. I can't stress this enough: Know the local market conditions before you purchase the property.

The second level of due diligence is the property condition, including physical items such as building systems, environmental matters and structural components. Just as important are the intangible items, such as title, survey, and zoning and land-use regulations.

Knowledge of contract law, insurance, finance, accounting, and tax law is also critical to doing things right at the beginning to ensure success at the end.

If you've never done it before, this is not a DIY project. The money you think you'll save by doing it yourself can cost twice as much to fix and may jeopardize the entire investment.

Admit what you don't know. Approach the property like an open-book test. If you don't know the answer to a question, find an expert who knows the answers.

Get accurate estimates from professionals of what it will cost to fix what is wrong. The time spent inspecting the property components is minimal and can save thousands of dollars in unexpected repairs.

The bottom-line is: Do your due diligence before you purchase your property. If you think it's expensive to hire a professional to do the job, wait until you hire an amateur.

Mistake 6: Misjudging Your Cash Flow

A careful eye on the cash flow will put more money in your pocket, give you more money to purchase other properties, and will allow you to become wealthier, faster.

Many real estate investors have fallen due to the lack of cash flow. This is the key phase for survival in the investing business. Not having cash reserves makes your position very risky and shaky. Sure, you can use your credit but credit needs repayment. And, that investment property will have hidden costs.

Think about it. The more pressure you're under, the easier it is to make silly mistakes. Make sure you allow for sufficient cash flow.

Lack of cash reserves puts unnecessary pressure on you to do substandard repairs, accept less than qualified tenants, and give into tenants' demands for fear of a vacancy.

When you have a sufficient cash reserves, you act rationally.

You hold out for a higher sales price.

You hold out for a qualified tenant.

You leave properties vacant rather than accepting unqualified tenants.

You call a tenant's bluff when they threaten to leave.

You take care of necessary repairs and improvements on your properties.

It's a whole different ball game than operating from a lack of cash. Buying properties with no money down isn't hard; it's handling the cash flow that's really hard. In other words, you can buy real estate without money; you just can't survive in the real estate business without cash reserves.

The bottom-line is: Consider accumulating cash reserves before investing in rental properties. If you don't have the cash flow, an asset can quickly become a huge liability.

Mistake 7: Not Screening Your Tenants

You should always screen your tenants. It is crucial to your survival as a landlord. The landlord who doesn't screen his tenants is the one who gets the worst tenants because the worst tenants can't get an apartment from anyone else because everyone else does a background check! Your primary concern is whether or not they have been evicted. If they have been evicted once, they know how to play the eviction game and will do it again.

If you have to evict a tenant, the process could take up to 6 months, depending on which state you live in. It takes longer to evict in most northern states than it does in the southern states.

Whether it is one month or six months, that is your cash flow! Once gone, it can never be recouped. Sure, you will probably be awarded that amount when you go through the eviction court but you will probably never collect it.

A check for evictions will cost you between $10 and $20, while a credit and criminal check costs more. But, don't pay this fee yourself. Instead, have the prospective tenant give you an application fee at the time that they apply for the apartment. This will cover your cost and if you set the application fee higher than the cost of the background check, you can make a little money, too!

The bottom-line is: Your biggest cost as a landlord is turnover. Every time you turn a unit over, you usually lose a month's rent, plus the maintenance or repair cost to get the unit back into shape. Be smart. Perform a background check on all of your prospective tenants. There are several nationwide services that provide background checks for landlords. Use them wisely.

Mistake 8: Paying Before Completion

Paying for a construction job before it is 100% complete gives the contractor no incentive to return to finish the job.

You'll get frustrated and angry as you waste your time chasing a contractor who is spending his time trying to finish jobs that he hasn't gotten paid for yet.

Even if he has the best of intentions, in his mind he is paid, and the job is done. He doesn't think twice about not showing up again, because he is now focused on his next paycheck. That's just the way they think.

The bottom-line is: Never make that last payment until the job is 100% complete – to your satisfaction. No matter how many promises he makes about coming back, no matter how small the task is that is left, no matter how much he needs the money. If you pay the contractor before the work is completely finished, just assume that you will have to finish the job yourself or pay someone else to finish the job!

Mistake 9: Paying Full Price for Late Work

You must always use written contracts when working with contractors. And, you should always have a late penalty clause that punishes the contractor a certain amount of money each day, usually $100.00 per day, when he does not finish on time.

This is how most construction companies work. The owner hustles around and gets as many jobs as he can. He then begins all of the new jobs as he is in the process of completing his old jobs.

At first, he pays you and your job enough attention to keep you happy. But soon, because he has been paying you attention and has not been taking care of his old customers, they become angry and start calling him. So, he runs back and does a little more work on their job, leaving your job unfinished.

Then, you get angry because he has not been at your job and now you are behind schedule. So he comes to your job for a couple of days and you are once again happy.

While there, he has picked up a couple more jobs and he goes there to start those jobs and makes those people happy.

Once again, you become angry so he comes to your job for a day. But, a day is the most he can spend because he has to go to his older customers who are even angrier than you. Can you see the cycle? The contractor goes from job to job trying to avoid the pain of unhappy customers.

The solution: Create pain for him in the form of a penalty clause. If the contractor is going to lose $100 a day for every day he is over his scheduled finish date on your job, do you think that it is sufficient pain to get him to complete on time? You bet it is!

You can waste your time calling him and leaving him nasty messages, sending him disgruntled letters, hunting him down at his other job sites. Do all this in an attempt to get him to finish your job, you may or may not be successful.

But, if you simply take money out of his pocket, you will have his full attention.

The bottom-line is: Always use a written contract on every construction job. And, always negotiate a penalty clause in every contract.

Mistake 10: Allowing Yourself to Burn Out

Many real estate investors get burned out and overwhelmed. They try to get their hands into everything and often don't see any results right away, so they spin in circles and ultimately burn out. Plus, it is easy to burn out if you're trying to do everything or trying to learn everything.

We all get so wrapped up in the thrill of real estate investing, once you start buying, selling and cashing those big checks, you will know what I am talking about, that it begins to become all encompassing.

We all have cell phones, so we do not miss a single call. When the phone rings at our home office, we go running like a bat out of hell from the dinner table because this could be the next big deal.

We take calls from contractors and suppliers at all hours and especially on Sunday nights. We allow tenants to have us at their beck and call because we fear that if we do not say "how high" when they say "jump," they might move out.

Before we know it, our lives are consumed with nothing else. We left our jobs so that we could stop working for the "man" and be our own boss. Now, we've come to realize that we are working for a boss who is much worse, a tyrant. That tyrant is us.

How does this happen? It happens because we do not effectively plan our businesses. One of the benefits that you will achieve from planning is you will be able to create systems and checklists to control your real estate investing business.

Once these systems and checklists are in place, you will know what needs to be done in any given situation. You will look at the checklist daily to review what has been accomplished and what still needs to be done.

You should have checklists for every aspect of your business. Here's an example of some key checklists:

a) Property Evaluation	buying right, market analysis, property analysis
b) Property Inspection	Room by room analysis, estimating repairs, formula worksheets
c) Contractor Management	bid process, contracts and agreements
d) Renovation Management	cash flow, required activities, scheduling, contractor management
e) Tenant Management	application process, background check, move-in process, leases and contracts

These are just a few of the many checklists and systems that you will need to create and use on a day-to-day basis so that you are running your business and your business is not running you.

One of the benefits of systems and checklists is that, as you grow your business and hire people to work for you, you will train them by teaching them how to use the checklists and systems. You will train them to complete the tasks associated with each system and checklist.

You will supervise them by revising the systems and checklists that they are working on. This is the fastest way to grow your business.

If you do not want to create all of those systems and checklists yourself, find someone who already has a successful real estate investing business and find out what they are using.

The bottom-line is: The sooner you systemize, the sooner you will be free to make choices based on what you want to do, instead of what your business needs you to do.

Mistake 11: Over-Improving Your Property

Anyone can renovate a house and have it come out looking like the Taj Mahal, but that will not put the most amount of money in our pockets.

You shouldn't cut corners or hide defects in a house. At the same time, if you are renovating a $75,000 house, you do not want to install real wood floors, marble countertops, stainless steel appliances, and replace the exterior siding with expensive brick and stone.

You want to do the repairs that will give you the biggest return for the money. If you are repairing a rental unit, you want to use materials that will last, like commercial tile floors for the kitchen and baths (instead of the 12 x 12 stick-ons), commercial grade carpet and counter tops that are designed to hide cuts and dirt.

If you are renovating a house for re-sale, you want to focus on the kitchen and baths. Spend all of your extra rehab money in these rooms because these are the rooms that will sell your house. They should be bright, clean and shiny.

Bring the house back to a like-new condition without making everything new.

It is amazing how a little paint and cleaning can change the appearance of a house or an apartment.

The bottom-line is: When planning your repairs, repair anything that is broken or outdated, but don't go around the house installing all new cabinets and counters if you do not need them. Remember, make it nice, put out a quality product, but at the same time, keep in mind that you are not going to live there and the people who buy the house are most likely going to make changes anyway.

Mistake 12: Being Underinsured

There are two sides to every real estate investment: Risk and reward. But, there is virtually no discussion of risk management in current real estate books or seminars. The only "risk management" the vast majority of real estate investors do is hope of the best.

Risk management in real estate is far more important than in the stock market because the risks in real estate far exceed those in the stock market – like getting sued and having to pay a judgment that is far more than the value of the property.

Insurance on rental property goes beyond insuring the building against fire or a hurricane. For example, you need to look at your own coverage for liability. If there's a loose railing and a tenant's child falls off a balcony, or there is a burglary and a tenant says it's because you wouldn't install security alarms, you're likely to get sued.

You spent all those hours studying those books and tapes, sifting through countless numbers of potential sellers, and inspecting every type of house imaginable.

Through your own persistence, you have put deal upon deal together, built a substantial portfolio of properties (not to mention a sizeable bank account), only to have some idiot sue you for something stupid and take it all away from you!

You should learn about asset protection just as diligently as you learn about real estate investing. You should NOT hold your properties in your name.

Think of it this way. If an attorney was doing an asset search with your name on it, he should come away thinking that you are a dead beat.

The bottom-line is: Each of your properties should be purchased in a trust or a corporation. Your bank accounts should also be in trusts. Your home, automobile, boats... should all be hidden in asset-protection devices. Speak with an asset-protection attorney to find out which asset protection vehicles you should be in. You have worked too hard for yourself and for your family to have some idiot come along and remove even one dime from your pockets.

Single Life Expectancy (for beneficiaries)

Age	Life Expectancy	Age	Life Expectancy
56	28.7	84	8.1
57	27.9	85	7.6
58	27.0	86	7.1
59	26.1	87	6.7
60	25.2	88	6.3
61	24.4	89	5.9
62	23.5	90	5.5
63	22.7	91	5.2
64	21.8	92	4.9
65	21.0	93	4.6
66	20.2	94	4.3
67	19.4	95	4.1
68	18.6	96	3.8
69	17.8	97	3.6
70	17.0	98	3.4
71	16.3	99	3.1
72	15.5	100	2.9
73	14.8	101	2.7
74	14.1	102	2.5
75	13.4	103	2.3
76	12.7	104	2.1
77	12.1	105	1.9
78	11.4	106	1.7
79	10.8	107	1.5
80	10.2	108	1.4
81	9.7	109	1.2
82	9.1	110	1.1
83	8.6	111 and over	1.0

GLOSSARY

AGI (Adjusted Gross Income) - Used to calculate federal income tax, AGI includes all the income you received over the course of the year such as wages, interest, dividends and capital gains minus things such as business expenses, contributions to a qualified IRA, moving expenses, alimony and capital losses.

Contribution - IRA contributions are limited to $3,000 a year for those younger than 50 and $3,500 a year for those 50 and older. Contributions are classified as either tax deductible or nondeductible.

Deductible/Nondeductible - Contributions to a traditional IRA are tax deductible if you are not covered by your employer's retirement plan. Even if you do participate in a company pension or 401(k) plan, you still may be able to deduct contributions to a traditional IRA depending upon your income and filing status. Contributions to a Roth IRA are not deductible.

Education IRA - In 2001, these plans were renamed the Coverdell Education Savings Account in honor of the late U.S. Senator Paul Coverdell. Individuals can make annual contributions of up to $2,000 per child into an account that's exclusively for helping to pay higher education costs. The money contributed to a Coverdell account doesn't count against the $3,000 ($3,500 if 50 and older) annual total individuals may contribute to their combined individual IRAs. The earnings and withdrawals from a Coverdell account are tax-free, but you can't deduct the contributions from your income tax.

IRA (Individual Retirement Account) - IRAs are retirement accounts with tax advantages. Individuals may contribute up to $3,000 ($3,500 if 50 or older) annually to an IRA as long as they have earned $3,000 in that year (i.e., you can't pad it with unearned money). The investment grows tax-free until it's withdrawn, usually after age 59½. Money withdrawn before age 59½ will usually get hit with a 10 percent penalty, but there are some exceptions.

MAGI (Modified Adjusted Gross Income) - For the purpose of determining their contribution limit, some people use their AGI increased by certain exclusions from their income. Examples of exclusions to income include foreign-earned income and housing costs of U.S. citizens or residents living abroad and income from sources within Puerto Rico, Guam or American Samoa.

Required Minimum Distribution - Generally, a traditional IRA owner must begin taking money out of the account by April 1 of the year after he or she turns 70½. The amount is a minimum distribution determined by the account holder's age and life expectancy. The IRS has established simplified tables that a traditional IRA owner can use to figure the required distribution. If required distributions are not made on time, the IRS will collect an excise tax. Roth IRAs aren't subject to minimum distribution requirements until after the Roth owner dies.

Rollover - This is the term used when transferring assets from one tax-deferred retirement plan to another.

Roth IRA - The most notable thing about a Roth is withdrawals are tax-free if the account has been open for at least five years and you're at least 59½ when you start to withdraw money. Contributions to a Roth are not tax deductible. The Roth is named for Senator William Roth, Jr., chairman of the Senate Finance Committee.

Tax and Penalty-Free Withdrawals - You can take money out of your IRA tax-free and penalty-free as long as you repay the full amount within 60 days. It's a good way to make an interest-free loan to yourself. You can only do this once every 12 months.

ABOUT THE AUTHOR

Michael Poggi is a nationally-recognized public speaker and professional investor, developer and author with over two decades of investing experience. Michael speaks on how to buy Real Estate in your IRA or old 401k plan. He teaches people how to make their IRA self-directed in the true sense so they can have greater control over their investments. He shows people how to make their IRA cash flow monthly, tax-free using real estate and other turnkey investment strategies.

In addition, Michael is the president and founder of The Millionaires Investment Group, based in Ft. Lauderdale, Florida. It is the largest commercial real estate group in the state of Florida, meeting on a monthly basis to network and partner on real estate ventures of all sizes. Michael's company specializes in many aspects of commercial real estate, vacant land, development projects, and foreclosed properties. The group also attracts top notch speakers from all around the country who are featured monthly to provide additional education to the group.

Michael is often a featured guest on the Money Talk radio shows. His company, Build Wealth with Land, LLC. is one of the largest land providers in the U.S., providing hundreds of vacant lots yearly to investors and builders.

Michael has bought and sold over 435 vacant lots and bank-owned houses in the last 10 years tax free.